Authoritarianism: A Very Short Introduction

VERY SHORT INTRODUCTIONS are for anyone wanting a stimulating and accessible way into a new subject. They are written by experts, and have been translated into more than 45 different languages.

The series began in 1995, and now covers a wide variety of topics in every discipline. The VSI library currently contains over 750 volumes—a Very Short Introduction to everything from Psychology and Philosophy of Science to American History and Relativity—and continues to grow in every subject area.

Very Short Introductions available now:

Available soon:

(TO BE CONFIRMED)

For more information visit our website

www.oup.com/vsi/

James Loxton

AUTHORITARIANISM

A Very Short Introduction

OXFORD
UNIVERSITY PRESS

Great Clarendon Street, Oxford, OX2 6DP,
United Kingdom

Oxford University Press is a department of the University of Oxford.
It furthers the University's objective of excellence in research, scholarship,
and education by publishing worldwide. Oxford is a registered trade mark of
Oxford University Press in the UK and in certain other countries

Published in the United States of America by Oxford University Press
198 Madison Avenue, New York, NY 10016, United States of America

British Library Cataloguing in Publication Data
Data available

Library of Congress Control Number: 2023952562

ISBN 978-0-19-287269-2

Printed and bound by
CPI Group (UK) Ltd, Croydon, CR0 4YY

Contents

Preface

"A spectre is haunting Europe—the spectre of Communism." With these famous words, Karl Marx and Friedrich Engels open their 1848 pamphlet *The Communist Manifesto*. Today another spectre is haunting the world: the spectre of authoritarianism. If concepts like anarchism, communism, fascism, and totalitarianism helped to define past ages, the great "ism" of our own is authoritarianism. While not a new term—or a new phenomenon—it has entered the popular lexicon like never before. The election of Donald Trump as president of the United States in 2016, and the violent storming of the U.S. Capitol on January 6, 2021, raised the previously unimaginable prospect of a slide into authoritarianism in the world's oldest democracy. And the rise of China has meant that, for the first time since the collapse of the Soviet Union, the world again has an authoritarian superpower. Authoritarianism in the 21st century is alive and well.

But what is it exactly? What distinguishes authoritarianism from democracy, and what forms does it take? How are authoritarian regimes born, and why do they sometimes die? Why are some more durable than others? What legacies do authoritarian regimes leave behind? These are the big questions that drive this book. Chapter 1 discusses how authoritarianism is defined and how this has changed over time. For better or worse, today authoritarianism simply means non-democracy. Chapter 2 shows that authoritarianism comes in different shapes and forms, including military, single-party, and personalist regimes. Some of them hold elections, but this does not make them democracies. To be a democracy, there must be universal suffrage, free and fair elections, and protection for civil liberties such as freedom of speech and freedom of assembly.

The next three chapters examine the "life cycle" of authoritarian regimes: birth, life, and death. Chapter 3 asks why democracy sometimes breaks down and is replaced by authoritarianism. It emphasizes the role of the "disloyal" and "semi-loyal" opposition, and shows how polarization and fear can cause people to turn against democracy. Chapter 4 examines four recurring problems in authoritarian regimes: the problem of legitimacy, the problem of information, the problem of frenemies, and the problem of succession. Chapter 5 considers the transition from authoritarianism to democracy, highlighting the importance of leadership and the international environment.

The final two chapters consider the persistence of authoritarian regimes and authoritarian legacies. Chapter 6 examines the puzzle of authoritarian durability, showing that factors such as oil, revolution, and cross-border cooperation have allowed some authoritarian regimes to withstand pressures for democratization more successfully than others. Chapter 7 concludes by looking at how legacies of authoritarianism may live on after a transition to democracy. These include not just the unhealed wound of human rights abuses, but also constitutions and political parties created by authoritarian officials—parties that often return to power in free and fair elections. For readers who wish to explore the topics covered in this book in more depth, the References and Further Reading sections provide a wealth of potential jumping-off points.

This book was written while on sabbatical at Oxford University during the fall of 2022 and as a visiting scholar at Princeton University during the spring of 2023. I am grateful to Nuffield

College and the Latin American Centre at the former, and the Program in Latin American Studies at the latter, for hosting me and providing the most conducive environments imaginable for writing. I am indebted to Steven Levitsky, Philipp Lehmann, Scott Phelps, Kenneth M. Roberts, Scott Mainwaring, and two anonymous reviewers for their invaluable comments on earlier drafts of the manuscript. I thank my editor at Oxford University Press, Luciana O'Flaherty, for guiding this project through to completion. This book is dedicated to Julieta Reyes Simpson and the rest of my Chilean family. May they never again have to live under authoritarianism.

List of illustrations

Chapter 1
What is authoritarianism?

Authoritarianism is a broad umbrella term for non-democratic systems of government, including military, single-party, and personalist regimes. It is hardly the first term to describe repressive forms of rule. Tyranny dates all the way back to ancient Greece. Dictatorship was an office in the Roman Republic, most famously held by self-proclaimed "dictator for life" Julius Caesar. Despotism was popularized by French philosophers in the 18th century. Authoritarianism, by contrast, is a more modern term—and one whose meaning has evolved over time.

According to the *Oxford English Dictionary*, the term *authoritarian* made its first appearance in the English language in 1856, referring to a "person who favours obedience to authority as opposed to personal liberty." It is still sometimes used in this way today, as with the concept of authoritarian parenting. After the Second World War, however, the term became more explicitly political. In 1950, for example, a group of scholars including the German philosopher Theodor W. Adorno published the book *The Authoritarian Personality*, in which they argued that some people possessed psychological traits that made them vulnerable to the appeal of movements like Nazism.

Today authoritarianism refers to a type of political regime. A regime is a set of rules, whether formal or informal, that determines how governments are formed and what those governments are allowed to do. Do leaders reach high office through free and fair elections in which all adults can vote, or do they take power through violence? Are basic rights like freedom of speech and freedom of assembly respected, or are critical media outlets shut down and members of the opposition harassed, imprisoned, or killed? The answers to such questions will vary dramatically depending on whether one lives in an authoritarian or democratic regime.

This chapter considers the concept of authoritarianism and how its meaning has evolved. It traces the current popularity of the term to a Spanish scholar named Juan J. Linz, who argued that authoritarian regimes should be distinguished from totalitarian regimes such as Nazi Germany and the Soviet Union. However, over the decades the definition of authoritarianism has broadened so that it now simply means non-democracy. While in theory this should make it easy to spot authoritarian regimes, in practice it is complicated by the fact that many of them claim to be democracies. We should not be fooled. To be a democracy, there must be universal suffrage, free and fair elections, and protection for civil liberties. If any of these is missing, the regime is authoritarian, not democratic.

Juan J. Linz: the father of authoritarianism

The years after the Second World War saw intense interest in a new political phenomenon: totalitarianism. The rise of the Nazis in Germany in the 1930s, and of Joseph Stalin in the Soviet Union at roughly the same time, seemed to signal something new and terrible in the world. In theory, Nazism and Stalinism were on opposite ends of the ideological spectrum. In practice, observers such as the German philosopher Hannah Arendt noticed striking parallels between the two, arguing in her 1951 book *The Origins of Totalitarianism* that they were different expressions of the same phenomenon. These regimes became infamous for their extreme violence. What truly set totalitarianism apart, however, was how it completely collapsed the distinction between public and private life. This was a world of secret police, indoctrination, and "thoughtcrime," as George Orwell called it in his classic dystopian novel, *Nineteen Eighty-Four* (1949). Worse still, the appeal of totalitarian movements seemed to be on the rise.

This was the environment into which the celebrated sociologist and political scientist Juan J. Linz, who played a bigger role than anybody else in developing and popularizing the term *authoritarianism*, stepped in the 1960s and 1970s. Because academics, like all people, are shaped by their upbringing, it is worth saying a few words about his background. Linz was born in 1926 in Bonn, Germany, to a Spanish mother and German father. In 1932, he moved to Spain with his mother, where he would spend his formative years. In 1936, the Spanish Civil War broke out, pitting mostly leftist Republican forces against conservative Nationalist forces under the leadership of General Francisco Franco. In 1939, after three years of intense fighting, the Nationalists won and established a new order: the Franco regime. It would remain in place for the next three and a half decades, ending only with Franco's death in 1975.

The Franco regime was right-wing and concentrated virtually unlimited power in the hands of its leader, who took the title of Caudillo (typically translated in English as "strongman"). The regime was extraordinarily violent, there were no meaningful elections, and opposition political parties were banned. For these reasons, the Franco regime was often compared to Nazi Germany and fascist Italy—and indeed, both Adolf Hitler and Benito Mussolini provided military assistance to Nationalist forces during the Spanish Civil War. However, there were also some notable differences. The Franco regime, in the words of one historian, was an "eclectic hodge-podge" of groups unhappy with the direction of the country during the Second Spanish Republic (1931–9), including Catholics, the military, and monarchists. And

1. Francisco Franco of Spain.

it was pragmatic, as evidenced by its decision to remain neutral during the Second World War. This was not a regime trying to create a brave new world; it was fundamentally conservative in nature.

Linz grew up and did his undergraduate studies in Franco's Spain, before leaving for the United States in 1950 to complete a Ph.D. at Columbia University. He would later become a professor at Yale University, authoring some of the most influential works on political regimes and regime transitions ever. At the time that Linz launched his career, totalitarianism dominated the study of regimes. However, as someone who had first-hand knowledge of the Franco regime—and who, because of his family background, also had a good understanding of German history and politics— Linz believed that this was not a useful framework for understanding Spain. The Franco regime was obviously not democratic, but it was not totalitarian either. It was something else.

The word that Linz used for that something else was authoritarianism.

Linz laid out this argument in an influential 1964 essay titled "An Authoritarian Regime: Spain" and in a 1975 book called *Totalitarian and Authoritarian Regimes*. Authoritarian regimes, he argued, had three major characteristics that set them apart from totalitarian regimes. First, they allowed for what he called "limited pluralism." Totalitarian regimes seek total control. Not only does the ruling party claim a monopoly on political activity, but it also seeks to penetrate all societal organizations, from labor unions and business associations to sports clubs and local choirs. Under democracy, the opposite is true: the freedom to organize is nearly unlimited. Authoritarian regimes, according to Linz, fall somewhere in the middle. While some groups suffer ruthless persecution, others are allowed to operate more or less freely. Of particular importance in Franco's Spain was the Catholic Church, which continued to enjoy broad autonomy. Over time, Linz argued, such limited pluralism could even give rise to what he called a "semi-opposition," with authoritarian officials tolerating certain forms of criticism.

If limited pluralism was the most distinctive aspect of authoritarian regimes, Linz argued that a close second was "demobilization." Totalitarian regimes do not want their citizens at home and disengaged. They want them to take an active part in the life of the nation—provided it is within the strict confines laid out by the regime. They should go on hikes with the Hitler Youth or the Vladimir Lenin All-Union Pioneer Organization (which replaced the banned Boy Scouts in Nazi Germany and the Soviet Union, respectively). They should attend mass rallies and cast their ballots in meaningless electoral rituals in which the ruling party wins 99 percent of the vote (as the Communist Party did in the Soviet Union in 1937 and the Nazi Party did in Germany in 1938). Authoritarian regimes, Linz argued, want something different from their citizens. They want them to keep their heads down and their mouths shut. They should focus on their private lives, not concern themselves with public affairs. If totalitarianism is for joiners, authoritarianism is for the apathetic.

The final characteristic of authoritarian regimes, according to Linz, was lack of ideology. Totalitarian regimes have utopian aspirations. They want to remake their societies based on a set of widely known principles. Sometimes those principles are monstrous on the face of it. Other times they are betrayed, as Orwell so brilliantly satirized in his 1945 novella *Animal Farm*. After the animals overthrow their human rulers to create a new order dedicated to the principle of "All animals are equal," the pigs who led the revolution rewrite it as "All animals are equal, but some are more equal than others." Authoritarian regimes, according to Linz, are different. They are animated by a fuzzy "mentality" rather than a full-blown ideology. Linz liked to illustrate this difference with a telling anecdote. In Nazi Germany, he said, it was common for people to receive a copy of Hitler's *Mein Kampf* as a wedding gift. In Spain, official editions of Franco's speeches existed, but they were hard to find and almost nobody had read them.

These characteristics made Franco's Spain, in Linz's view, fundamentally different from cases such as Nazi Germany and the Soviet Union. It was authoritarian, not totalitarian. Over the years, Linz developed an intricate system of regime classification, including "traditional" regimes (which claim the right to rule on the basis of some timeless tradition), "sultanistic" regimes (overwhelmingly dominated by an individual or family and based on little more than bribery and fear), and "post-totalitarian" regimes (the fate of most totalitarian regimes as the decades pass and people stop believing in the official ideology). Each of these, Linz argued, was its own unique regime type, as different from the others as it was from democracy.

What was Linz's legacy? Perhaps the biggest was to change the language of politics itself. While he did not coin the term authoritarianism (Arendt, for example, occasionally used it in her writings), it was largely because of him that it is now as widely used as it is. But his impact was much broader. Although we no longer use the term authoritarianism as Linz defined it—and even less, beyond small specialist circles, do we use the other categories that he developed, such as sultanism—his fine-grained analysis of non-democratic regimes had a profound impact on generations of scholars. He helped to make such regimes legitimate objects of study, and inspired people to ask hard questions about why they were born and why they sometimes died. For these reasons, it is no exaggeration to describe Linz as the father of authoritarianism.

Authoritarianism as non-democracy

Authoritarianism today is defined not in contrast to totalitarianism, as it was for Linz, but in contrast to democracy. For better or worse, it is now used as shorthand for all non-democratic regimes. In his 2012 book *The Politics of Authoritarian Rule*, for example, the Yale University political scientist Milan Svolik defines an authoritarian regime as one that "fails to satisfy at least one of the following two criteria for democracy: (1) free and competitive legislative elections and (2) an executive that is elected either directly in free and competitive presidential elections or indirectly by a legislature in parliamentary systems." In other words, if a country's leaders are not chosen in free and fair elections, the regime is authoritarian. This broad understanding is also used by public figures, as when U.S. President Joe Biden spoke in his 2022 State of the Union Address about "the battle between democracy and autocracy." (Authoritarianism and autocracy are synonyms. They are used interchangeably.) In short, authoritarianism is the opposite of democracy. This is what authoritarianism means today, and this is how it is used in this book.

Why this change in our understanding of authoritarianism? One reason is that totalitarianism has largely disappeared. Nazi Germany died with Hitler in 1945, and Stalin's death in 1953 triggered a process of "de-Stalinization" in which the worst excesses of Soviet politics were curbed. Arguably the only truly totalitarian regime left in the world today is North Korea, in place since 1948. All independent organizations are banned and perceived disloyalty can result in torture, forced labor, or execution. Periodic elections are held in which official regime candidates win 100 percent of the vote. And a homegrown ideology mixing communism, militarism, and worship of the Kim dynasty (currently on its third generation) dominates all decision-making. Because of its isolation from the rest of the world, North Korea is sometimes called the "Hermit Kingdom." It would be just as accurate to describe it as a time capsule.

If totalitarianism has mostly vanished, democracy has become increasingly widespread. Historically, democracy has been rare. The country usually considered to be the first modern democracy is the United States, which, after winning independence in 1783, installed a regime based on competitive elections and then gradually moved toward universal suffrage. The number of democracies ebbed and flowed over the next two centuries, but always remained a clear minority. This began to change in the mid-1970s, however, with the onset of what the political scientist Samuel P. Huntington called the "third wave" of democratization. The third wave was a worldwide phenomenon: it began in southern Europe, before spreading to Latin America and parts of Asia, Africa, and post-communist Europe. In 1973, only about a quarter of the world's countries were democracies; by the late 1990s, more than half were. This has remained the case, more or less, ever since.

This growth in the number of democracies was accompanied by an ideological shift. While it is often treated as a uniquely legitimate form of government, democracy faced serious competition for much of the 20th century. This was especially true during the Cold War, when each of the world's superpowers, the United States and the Soviet Union, claimed to represent the best economic and political model. The Soviet model of state planning and single-party rule was seen by many as a viable alternative to the U.S. model of capitalism and democracy. The fall of the Berlin Wall in 1989 put an end to this. This led to not only the disappearance of many of the world's communist regimes—including the Soviet Union itself, which collapsed in 1991—but also the defeat of communism in the contest of ideas. The Cold War was over, and communism had lost. This is what the political scientist Francis Fukuyama meant when he wrote in a controversial 1992 book about "the end of history." He did not mean that nothing would ever happen again. He meant that democracy no longer had a serious ideological rival.

These three factors—the decline of totalitarianism, an explosion in the number of democracies, and the discrediting of communist ideology—all contributed to our current understanding of authoritarianism. In a world in which roughly half of all countries are democracies and roughly half are not, it makes sense to have a word for the non-democracies. That word is authoritarianism. Understood in this way, authoritarianism casts a wide net. It encompasses everything from communism to fascism, military rule to absolute monarchy, formal one-party regimes to those that hold somewhat competitive elections. While democracies also differ among themselves (e.g., some have presidential systems, while others have parliamentary systems), authoritarian regimes are a much more varied bunch. The major varieties of authoritarianism will be explored in Chapter 2. Nevertheless, the simple fact of not being a democracy turns out to yield a set of common challenges for authoritarian rulers, as discussed in Chapter 4. What is more, despite their differences, authoritarian regimes often recognize one another as kindred spirits, engaging in various forms of cross-border cooperation, as discussed in Chapter 6.

How to spot an authoritarian regime

If authoritarianism today means non-democracy, how do we know it when we see it? One thing we should *not* do is take regimes' self-classification at face value. There is a long history of authoritarian regimes insisting that they are, in fact, democracies. The Soviet Union claimed to practice "democratic centralism." The People's Republic of China, under the Chinese Communist Party, describes itself as a "socialist consultative democracy." The ruling party of Eritrea, a small country in the Horn of Africa and home to one of the world's most repressive regimes, is called the People's Front for Democracy and Justice. Some even incorporate these claims into their countries' names: the official name of communist East Germany was the German Democratic Republic, and the official name of North Korea is the Democratic People's Republic of Korea. A good rule of thumb is that if a regime puts "democratic" in its name, it isn't.

A seemingly more promising route is to ask whether a regime holds elections. This, too, can be deeply misleading. Some of the worst regimes in history have held elections, including Nazi Germany and the Soviet Union. Today, many authoritarian regimes even allow for a degree of multi-party competition. Take the example of Russia under Vladimir Putin. After Putin became president in 1999, Russia continued to hold regular elections for the presidency and legislature with the nominal participation of opposition parties. These became increasingly farcical, however. Putin's most serious rivals were barred from running, jailed, or assassinated—or, in the case of Alexei Navalny, all three (he survived a 2020 assassination attempt, before dying in an Arctic penal colony in 2024). Journalists were murdered. Independent media outlets were shut down. The right to protest was effectively abolished. Putin grew so powerful that he was often likened to the tsars of yesteryear—including, occasionally, by Putin himself. The case of contemporary Russia is a powerful illustration of what is known as the "electoralist fallacy." Elections are a necessary part of democracy, but they are not sufficient. They can be, and often are, utilized by authoritarian regimes.

So how, then, do we spot a democracy—and, by extension, an authoritarian regime? There is in fact a consensus among political scientists about how to define democracy. Democracy is a type of regime in which governments are chosen in free and fair elections with universal adult suffrage, and in which citizens enjoy a broad array of civil liberties, including freedom of speech, freedom of association, and freedom of assembly. This is known as the "procedural minimum definition of democracy." This definition is not about outcomes, such as whether a country is equal or unequal, corrupt or uncorrupt, orderly or chaotic. Some democracies are well governed; others are not. (The same is true of authoritarian regimes.) This definition is about the procedures used to choose governments and hold them accountable.

The influential political scientist Robert A. Dahl framed this view of democracy in terms of two key dimensions: "public contestation" and "inclusion." Public contestation is the right to challenge the government of the day. The most obvious way to challenge the government is to use one's vote to "throw the bums out," as the old saying goes. But contestation is about more than just voting. In a democracy, one can also publish op-eds against the bums, mock the bums on social media, form new organizations to challenge the bums, and march in the streets against them. The second dimension, inclusion, is about who possesses these rights. In a democracy, all adult citizens possess them, not just one class, gender, or ethnicity. If either public contestation or inclusion is significantly limited, the regime is authoritarian, not democratic.

Sometimes both public contestation and inclusion are absent, as in the case of the People's Republic of China. Since the 1949 Chinese Communist Revolution, the country has been under the single-party rule of the Chinese Communist Party. There are no competitive elections for national office. There is no freedom of speech, association, or assembly. Censorship is the norm, surveillance is ubiquitous, and criticism of the government can be met with severe punishment. While China began to loosen economic restrictions after 1978, it remained highly repressive in its politics. After Xi Jinping became the country's top leader in 2012, repression grew even worse. New forms of high-tech control were introduced, there was a clampdown on organized groups, and in the province of Xinjiang alone over a million people were detained. The persecution of the Uyghur ethnic minority in this province was so extreme that it may have amounted to "crimes against humanity," according to the United Nations. There is no ambiguity about how to classify China. It is an out-and-out authoritarian regime.

In other cases, only one of these two dimensions—public contestation and inclusion—is missing. That is still enough to make a regime authoritarian. Take the example of South Africa. Between 1948 and the early 1990s, the country was under the system of apartheid, which means "separateness" in Afrikaans. Apartheid placed severe restrictions on South Africa's non-white majority, determining where they could live, what kind of work they could do, whom they could marry, and much more. It also denied them the right to vote and run for office. Yet this was not a regime like communist China. For the country's white minority, it looked and felt a lot like democracy. There were regular multi-party elections and few limits on whites' freedom to say and do as they pleased. There was, in other words, a high degree of public contestation. However, because inclusion was so egregiously lacking, apartheid South Africa was authoritarian, not democratic.

Today it is less common to place formal limits on inclusion. However, authoritarian regimes still routinely limit public contestation. One option is to undermine the electoral process. Sometimes this happens in the run-up to the election, as in the case of contemporary Nicaragua. During the 2021 presidential election, the country's autocrat, Daniel Ortega, jailed a whopping seven opposition candidates. Nicaraguans were free to vote—as long as they voted for Ortega. Other times it happens on election day itself. One notorious example is the 1988 presidential election in Mexico, which by then had been under single-party rule for over half a century. When early results showed the main opposition candidate ahead, the computer system used to tabulate votes mysteriously crashed. One week later the official results showed that the government candidate had won. The president at the time of the election later admitted that it had been rigged.

Public contestation can also be undermined by limiting civil liberties. No country grants its citizens absolute freedom. In

2. **Illegal public assembly in Singapore.**

democracies, free speech often excludes violent and hateful rhetoric, permits to hold protests are sometimes denied, and new parties wishing to get on the ballot may face bureaucratic obstacles. The restrictions in authoritarian regimes, however, are of a different order of magnitude. A good example is Singapore. Since becoming independent in 1965, the small country has been governed without interruption by the People's Action Party, or PAP. It holds regular multi-party elections with universal suffrage, which the PAP always wins. But the regime does not steal elections outright. It relies on more subtle methods, such as the aggressive use of defamation laws, tight controls on the media, and restrictions on freedom of speech and assembly. In 2020, the Singaporean activist Jolovan Wham drew attention to the absence of basic rights in his country by holding up a piece of cardboard with a hand-drawn smiley face on it for a few seconds in front of a police station. He was promptly dragged before a court and charged with illegal public assembly. If citizens cannot openly challenge their government, they are living in an authoritarian regime.

Chapter 2
Varieties of authoritarianism

Authoritarian regimes come in many shapes and forms. One way they differ is in terms of ideology. Some are right-wing; others are left-wing. It can be hard for ideologues to accept this fact, either justifying or turning a blind eye to authoritarian regimes on their side of the aisle. Many on the left continue to defend Cuba's decades-old communist regime, despite its heavy-handed repression and prohibition on opposition activity of all kinds. In July 2021, after mass protests broke out across the island, the authorities responded by sentencing hundreds of protesters to prison sentences of up to twenty-five years—some of them mere teenagers. Many conservatives during the Cold War likewise overlooked the brutality of anti-communist regimes in places like Chile, South Africa, and Taiwan.

Another way that authoritarian regimes differ is in their levels of violence. All authoritarian regimes, by definition, repress their populations in ways that would be unacceptable in a democracy. Beyond this, however, they vary tremendously. At one extreme is Spain. During the Spanish Civil War (1936–9), both sides carried out atrocities. At war's end, the victorious Nationalists did not let bygones be bygones. They unleashed a vicious campaign of retribution, executing at least 20,000 Republican prisoners. At the opposite extreme is Portugal, which was under an authoritarian regime known as the Estado Novo (New State) between 1933 and 1974. Yet while the Estado Novo and Franco's Spain were similar in many ways, the former was much less deadly: the number of people killed in Portugal for political reasons was most likely in the low hundreds, not tens of thousands.

However, even if knowing a regime is authoritarian tells us little about its ideology or level of violence, this does not mean that each is totally unique. Most authoritarian regimes belong to one of three major subtypes: military, single-party, and personalist. The boundaries between them are not airtight. Indonesia's New Order regime from 1966 to 1998, for example, combined military rule, the personalist leadership of General Suharto, and an official party known as Golkar. There are also cases that do not fit into any of these categories, such as contemporary Iran. Since the 1979 Islamic Revolution, it has been a theocracy, or a regime in which religious leaders hold ultimate power. Nevertheless, military, single-party, and personalist regimes so dominate the authoritarian landscape that we can think of them as The Big Three. This chapter discusses each in turn, before examining the surprising tendency of authoritarian regimes in recent decades to allow a degree of multi-party competition.

Military regimes

The first of The Big Three is military rule. Military regimes have two core characteristics. First, they come to power through a coup d'état. The term comes from French and can be roughly translated as a "blow against the state." It would be more accurate, though, to say that it is a blow against *part* of the state by *another* part of the state. Specifically, it is when the military illegally overthrows a civilian leader. Coups are not a thing of the past. While they have become less common over time, they still happen. In Thailand, for example, the military seized power in 2014, the latest of many coups in the country's history. In Egypt, the military toppled the country's first-ever democratically elected president in 2013.

Some coups are bloodier than others. The most recent coup in Thailand was what is known as a "bloodless coup," where the military removes a civilian leader without violence. In Egypt, by contrast, the military massacred hundreds of supporters of the deposed president.

The second core characteristic of military regimes is that they involve some form of collective rule by the armed forces. These are not regimes like those of army commander Idi Amin in Uganda, who, after seizing power in a coup in 1971, declared himself "Lord of All the Beasts of the Earth and Fishes of the Sea" (as well as, famously, the "Last King of Scotland"). In military regimes, power is shared among officers rather than concentrated in the hands of one man. This is typically reflected in the formation of a junta, which means "board" or "committee" in Spanish. A military junta, then, is a committee of military officers. This does not mean that all decisions are made collectively. The junta will often appoint a president, much like a corporate board will appoint a CEO. However, while the president may be given wide latitude to run the country, he is ultimately answerable to the junta. And just like a corporate board and a CEO may end up butting heads, conflict sometimes breaks out between the junta and the president. In extreme cases, there may even be a "palace coup," in which parts of the military overthrow the regime's top leader while leaving the fundamentals of the regime intact.

A good illustration of how military regimes work is Argentina. During the 20th century, the country suffered repeated coups and bouts of military rule. Its last military regime was also its worst: in power from 1976 to 1983, it committed shocking human rights abuses, murdering and torturing its citizens on a mass scale. But who was in charge during these seven years? The fact that most readers will not know the answer to this question is not a coincidence: even by military regime standards, this was a highly collective form of rule. After taking power in a coup, the Argentine army, navy, and air force set up a junta in which the heads of each

3. Military junta in Argentina.

had a seat. The three branches then wrote up an explicit agreement in which each was guaranteed one-third of government positions, from the cabinet all the way down. During its seven years in power, the military regime cycled through a whopping four presidents and three interim presidents.

In addition to not being a thing of the past, military rule is not confined to any one region. In Latin America, nearly two-thirds of all countries were under military rule in the late 1970s. Greece was ruled by the military from 1967 to 1974. Africa's most populous country, Nigeria, was under military rule for all but a handful of years between 1966 and 1999, and a wave of coups in the early 2020s in the so-called "Coup Belt" led to military rule in countries including Mali, Niger, and Gabon. Several Asian countries have had military regimes, such as South Korea, Pakistan, and Myanmar (formerly Burma). The latter has been under military rule for most of the period since 1962. While the Burmese military began to give up some power to civilians after 2015, it reversed course in 2021, launching a coup and taking back full control.

Single-party regimes

The second major subtype of authoritarianism is single-party rule. Most readers of this book will be familiar with parties as they exist in democracies. Political parties under democracy are teams of politicians who compete for elected office under a shared label. Each party, as the word implies, is just one *part* of the political system, not the whole. Whether a country has a two-party system, as in the United States, or a multi-party system, as in most European countries, it is taken for granted that turnover in government will be a regular occurrence. "Democracy," as the political scientist Adam Przeworski memorably put it, "is a system in which parties lose elections." Single-party rule is the opposite: it is a system in which parties do *not* lose elections. Either the ruling party does not hold multi-party elections at all, or it holds them but then puts its thumb on the scale so that it always wins.

The strictest version of single-party rule—where all opposition parties are illegal—is most closely associated with communist regimes. This is no coincidence. The most important theorist of the role of parties in non-democratic settings was Vladimir Lenin, the first leader of the Soviet Union. Although fully committed to Marx's vision of a communist society, Lenin believed that the working class would never rise up and overthrow the capitalist order on its own. To help the process along, he argued, what was needed was a small group of professional revolutionaries organized into a "vanguard party." In the Russian Revolution of 1917, it was Lenin's Bolshevik Party that played this vanguard role. After taking power, the Bolsheviks became the Communist Party of the Soviet Union, the country's sole legal party. In the years after the Second World War, single-party communist regimes came to power throughout Eastern Europe, as well as in countries such as China, Vietnam, and Cuba.

A second, less restrictive version of single-party rule is what is known as a "hegemonic-party regime." These regimes do not ban opposition parties outright. They allow them to exist and even to participate in elections, but then use fraud, coercion, and other unfair advantages to make sure they always lose. One example is Mexico. Between 1929 and 2000, the country was governed by the Institutional Revolutionary Party, or PRI. Like the Communist Party of the Soviet Union, the PRI came to power after a revolution (the Mexican Revolution of 1910–20). But unlike the Soviet Union, Mexico's authoritarian regime held regular multi-party elections. These elections were not democratic. PRI presidential candidates won by implausibly high margins, and the opposition was not allowed to get anywhere near power. It took over a half-century before an opposition party was even allowed to win a governorship, much less the presidency. However, for the casual observer, the regime looked basically democratic, leading the Peruvian novelist Mario Vargas Llosa to describe it as "the perfect dictatorship."

Personalist and military regimes also sometimes create official ruling parties. However, these do not play the same central role as in single-party regimes. Brazil's last military regime (1964–85), for example, created a party called the National Renewal Alliance, or ARENA, which served as its official vehicle in undemocratic elections. ARENA had little real power, however. True single-party regimes are different. The most important symbol of the party's power in communist regimes is the Politburo, a contraction of the words "Political" and "Bureau." Much like the junta in a military regime, the Politburo is a committee of top party leaders that has the final word on government decisions. This is not to say that relations between the Politburo and the regime's top leader are always smooth. Just as there can be palace coups in military regimes, there can be bitter infighting in single-party regimes, replete with purges, show trials, and executions, as there were in the Soviet Union. But the party cannot simply be ignored. It is a real actor with real power.

Personalist regimes

Finally, there are personalist regimes. A personalist regime, as the name implies, is one that is dominated by a single person. The principle underlying such regimes is the one attributed to Louis XIV, the absolutist king of France: "L'état, c'est moi" ("I am the state"). Here the ruler's power is not checked by a military junta or committee of top party leaders. His word is law, the military is his goon squad, and the treasury is his personal bank account. These regimes often construct a cult of personality around the leader. The state-controlled media is flooded with accounts of his heroic deeds. Statues of him dominate public spaces. Citizens are required to praise him in obsequious and sometimes bizarre language, such as "father," "gallant knight," and even "premier pharmacist" in the case of Syria's late ruler, Hafez al-Assad (he was not a pharmacist). The regime of Rafael Trujillo (1930–61) in the Dominican Republic went even further, changing the name of the capital from Santo Domingo to Ciudad Trujillo.

This concentration of power in the hands of one person distinguishes personalist regimes from military regimes. This does not mean that the military plays no role. Such regimes, in fact, are often born of coups. One example is the regime of Joseph Mobutu in the Democratic Republic of the Congo, who during his three decades in power earned a well-deserved reputation for being one of the most corrupt leaders in history. (He later changed his name to Mobutu Sese Seko, and the name of his country to Zaire.) In 1960, just months after gaining its independence from Belgium, the country suffered its first coup at the hands of Colonel Mobutu, the head of the Congolese army. Five years later, he carried out a second coup, this time taking power for himself. The resulting regime was personalist in the extreme: its official ideology was "Mobutism," and Mobutu was given honorifics such as "Redeemer," "Father of the Nation," and even "Messiah." Like Hafez al-Assad, who was later replaced by his son, Bashar,

4. Mobutu Sese Seko on a Zairean banknote.

Mobutu reportedly planned for his son, Nyiwa, to succeed him. However, the son died before the handover could take place, and Mobutu was overthrown in 1997.

Other personalist regimes are born at the hands not of a military leader but of a democratically elected one. This is known as a "self-coup." The distinguishing feature of a self-coup is that, unlike a normal coup, the civilian leader is not the victim of an illegal power grab, but its perpetrator. (This is reflected in some of the other terms used for it, such as executive coup, executive takeover, or presidential coup.) One example is Ferdinand Marcos in the Philippines. Marcos was elected president in 1965 and then re-elected four years later. Not wanting to step down after the end of his constitutionally mandated two-term limit, he carried out a self-coup by declaring martial law in 1972. Congress was shut, opponents were arrested or killed, and critical media were silenced. The country came under the firm control of Marcos and his wife Imelda, whose close political partnership was described by one former regime insider as a "conjugal dictatorship." During this time, the couple amassed an extraordinary fortune—as famously symbolized by Imelda's 3,000 pairs of shoes—before being forced from power in 1986.

As these examples illustrate, family members often play an important role in personalist regimes. Indeed, another name for them is "family dictatorships," which in some cases become multi-generational dynasties. The personalist regime of the Somoza family in Nicaragua, for example, was established in 1936 and lasted until 1979, with the baton first passing from father to son, and then from brother to brother. In Haiti, the regime of François "Papa Doc" Duvalier was established in 1957, with power then handed to his son, Jean-Claude "Baby Doc" Duvalier, who ruled until 1986. And, of course, there are absolute monarchies like Saudi Arabia, Brunei in Southeast Asia, and Eswatini (formerly Swaziland) in southern Africa, where hereditary succession is even more explicit. Whether monarchies such as these should be grouped together with regimes in which hereditary succession is informal, as in the cases of Nicaragua and Haiti, is debatable. Much of it ultimately comes down to how seriously one takes the idea of royal bloodlines. At the very least, the two forms of rule bear a strong family resemblance.

The new authoritarianism?

The Big Three are alive and well. A time-traveling political scientist from a half-century ago would still recognize much of what she saw in the world today: military, single-party, and personalist regimes continue to dominate the authoritarian landscape. Some things, however, would be new. The biggest change she would observe is the widespread use of multi-party elections. Historically, it has been rare for authoritarian regimes to carry out such elections. Today it is the norm. Even more surprising is the fact that these elections often involve a degree of real competition. The political scientists Steven Levitsky and Lucan Way call this "competitive authoritarianism." This is where elections are not a complete and utter farce, but they are not free and fair either. There might be fraud, but it is limited fraud. There might be coercion, but it is limited coercion. Elections are a hard-fought affair in which victory cannot be taken for granted.

As Levitsky and Way put it: "In competitive authoritarian regimes, incumbents are forced to sweat." While they nearly always win, their margins of victory are usually small enough to seem plausible. This is authoritarianism with deniability.

A good example of competitive authoritarianism is Peru. In 1990, Alberto Fujimori, a political outsider of Japanese descent, was democratically elected president. In 1992, he carried out a self-coup: with the support of the military, he dissolved Congress, purged the courts, and arrested opposition politicians. Fujimori's initial plan was to establish full-blown authoritarianism. However, in the face of an international backlash, he decided to restore the outward trappings of democracy. For the next eight years, his government held regular presidential and legislative elections, while using a range of dirty tricks to stay in power. The electoral authorities were filled with cronies. Disobedient judges were dismissed. The media was bought off. And constitutional term limits were ignored, with Fujimori running for—and winning, through fraud—an illegal third term in 2000. It was only after a series of leaked videos revealed the extent of corruption under Fujimori that his regime collapsed.

The Fujimori regime was not unique. Between 1990 and 2019, around 15 percent of all countries were competitive authoritarian at any given time. While such regimes could be found in several regions, they were especially common in Sub-Saharan Africa and the post-communist world. One example is Russia under Boris Yeltsin. A former Communist Party official, Yeltsin was elected president in 1991. While his decade in office would become the high-water mark for Russian freedom, his rule was not really democratic. Like Fujimori in Peru, Yeltsin carried out a self-coup in 1993, even using tanks to shell his opponents in parliament. He abused state resources and engaged in fraud. In 1999, Yeltsin transferred power to his handpicked successor, Vladimir Putin, who went on to impose an even harsher form of authoritarian rule.

The path to competitive authoritarianism has changed over time. In the 1990s, competitive authoritarian regimes typically emerged from one-party regimes under pressure from the United States and its allies to democratize. They responded by allowing multi-party elections, but not a level playing field. Today the most common path is the opposite: it is the product not of authoritarian regimes opening up, but of democratic regimes closing down. Here so-called "populists" often play a pivotal role. These are politicians who claim to be champions of the common people against the corrupt elite. They present themselves as outsiders and promise to take a hammer to the establishment. Once in office, they often make good on their anti-establishment promises by stacking the courts, silencing independent media, and hounding the opposition. By the time the dust has settled, the country is no longer democratic. It is competitive authoritarian.

Peru's Fujimori was a pioneer of this populist path to competitive authoritarianism. More recent examples include Hugo Chávez in Venezuela, Recep Tayyip Erdoğan in Turkey, and Viktor Orbán in Hungary, who, after coming to power in 1999, 2003, and 2010, respectively, used the power of the state to tilt the playing field in their favor. The election of Narendra Modi of the Hindu nationalist Bharatiya Janata Party, or BJP, as prime minister of India in 2014 seemed to put the world's largest democracy on a similar path. Modi's persecution of the media, NGOs, and political opponents led one prominent research institute in 2021 to reclassify India as an "electoral autocracy." Donald Trump's election as U.S. president in 2016 prompted fears that the United States might suffer a similar fate. Trump's two-month effort to overturn the results of the 2020 presidential election after his defeat—culminating in the violent storming of the U.S. Capitol by his supporters on January 6, 2021—showed that these fears were well founded, even if this undemocratic power grab ultimately failed.

There are some historical precedents for competitive authoritarianism. In Argentina, the election of former coup leader Juan Perón in 1946 led to the establishment of a competitive authoritarian regime until his overthrow in 1955. Malaysia was under the competitive authoritarian rule of one party, the United Malays National Organisation, or UMNO, for approximately six decades after gaining independence in 1957. There is no doubt, however, that competitive authoritarianism has become more common. In an odd sense, this marks a victory for democracy. Competitive authoritarian regimes are hypocritical: they pretend to be democracies, but they are not democracies. And hypocrisy, as the saying goes, is the compliment that vice pays to virtue. In today's world, even many authoritarian regimes feel they must pretend to be democracies.

What is less clear is whether this represents a new type of "hybrid regime" blurring the lines between democracy and authoritarianism, or simply a new set of practices employed by The Big Three. Many of the regimes classified as competitive authoritarian could be comfortably slotted into one of these categories. The Fujimori regime was thoroughly personalist. In countries like Cambodia and Mozambique, the ruling parties of one-party regimes made a smooth transition to competitive elections—but not democracy—in the 1990s. In Thailand, even the military has entered the mix. After seizing power in a coup in 2014, its new rulers held competitive elections in 2019. The head of the Thai junta managed to retain his position as prime minister thanks to made-to-order electoral rules and likely fraud. In short, while the shift toward multi-party elections would strike our time-traveling political scientist as noteworthy, she would still find much about the world's authoritarian landscape familiar.

Chapter 3
The birth of authoritarian regimes

Where do authoritarian regimes come from? One answer is to go back to the shift that began approximately 12,000 years ago from small hunter-gatherer societies, which tended to be highly egalitarian and to choose their leaders by group consensus, to large-scale ones based on agriculture, virtually all of which were authoritarian until very recently. Even ancient Athens would not qualify as a democracy by modern standards: only 10–20 percent of its inhabitants were citizens and thus allowed to participate in politics, and there was no protection for individual civil liberties. Its most famous citizen, Socrates, was sentenced to death for the crimes of corrupting the youth and not holding the right religious views. And women, the foreign-born (and their descendants), and the city-state's many slaves were shut out of the political process altogether.

Another answer is to say that authoritarian regimes beget new authoritarian regimes. Because authoritarianism comes in different shapes and forms, it is possible—in fact, common—for one type to replace another. The Russian Revolution of 1917, for example, replaced Russia's monarchy with a communist regime. In Ethiopia, the long-ruling Emperor Haile Selassie was overthrown in a coup in 1974 and later killed. The monarchy was replaced by a far-left military regime known as the Derg. The Derg, in turn, was overthrown by rebels in 1991, leading to the establishment of a new single-party regime. In this way, Ethiopia underwent two separate regime changes in less than twenty years—without ever becoming a democracy.

But the path to authoritarianism that is likely to be of most interest to readers of this book is democratic breakdown. This means not just a change of government, but the collapse of the democratic regime itself. Here the birth of authoritarianism and the death of democracy go hand in hand.

Democratic breakdown can happen in one of two ways: at the hands of the military (coup), or at the hands of an elected leader (self-coup), as discussed in Chapter 2. The most famous example of a self-coup is Germany after the Nazis came to power in 1933. Starting as a small party in the 1920s, the Nazi Party grew increasingly popular with German voters, eventually becoming the most-voted-for party in two consecutive parliamentary elections in 1932. This allowed Adolf Hitler to become chancellor—and

5. **Chancellor Adolf Hitler prior to his 1933 self-coup.**

from there, to dismantle democracy from within. An example of democratic breakdown at the hands of the military is Chile. In 1970, following decades of stable electoral competition, a leftist named Salvador Allende was elected president. Three years later, the military overthrew him in a coup, leading to seventeen years of military rule under the leadership of General Augusto Pinochet.

In addition to the coup/self-coup distinction, the speed of democratic breakdown varies. Military coups tend to happen in one fell swoop. Self-coups, by contrast, can play out either quickly or slowly. Sometimes an elected leader comes to power, then calls the tanks into the streets and gives himself absolute power. Other times the power grab is more gradual. The leader might start out by tinkering with the courts and the electoral authorities, then begin to exert greater control over the media, then bit by bit increase the level of repression against opponents, until finally— possibly years later—people wake up to discover that they no longer live in a democracy. We can think of the first scenario as decapitation. The second is death by a thousand cuts.

What explains the breakdown of democracy? A good place to start, once again, is with the work of Juan J. Linz. This chapter examines Linz's concepts of the "disloyal" and "semi-loyal" opposition, and highlights the uncomfortable fact that democratic breakdown is often supported—or at least tolerated—by a significant portion of the population. It considers how polarization and fear can cause people to turn against democracy, and illustrates the importance of these factors through the examples of Germany and Chile.

Disloyal and semi-loyal opposition

Two key actors must be considered when thinking about the death of democracy: those who kill it, and those who fail to save it. In a slim, pioneering book from 1978, Juan J. Linz called these actors the "disloyal" and "semi-loyal" opposition. Both are a riff on the concept of the loyal opposition, a British term that captures a critical idea: one can oppose a particular government while remaining loyal to the democratic regime. Thus, when Britain's Conservative Party is in power, the Labour Party does everything it can to criticize its policies, draw attention to its scandals, and hold it to account more broadly. But it does not try to instigate a coup or provoke a violent uprising. It is fully supportive of the democratic system, secure in the knowledge that it is always just one election away from potentially forming government.

The disloyal opposition is different: these are actors who oppose not just the government of the day, but democracy itself. All democracies have disloyal actors. They vary tremendously, however, in their level of influence. The most obviously disloyal actors are terrorist, guerrilla, or other violent groups. Take the example of Germany. During the period known as the Weimar Republic (1918–33), the country's young democracy was rocked by street battles between paramilitary groups attached to various political parties, most famously the Nazi Stormtroopers, or SA. These groups beat up, intimidated, and sometimes killed their enemies. If we fast-forward several decades, we also find political violence in (West) Germany, this time in the form of a far-left group called the Red Army Faction, or RAF. During the 1970s, the group carried out assassinations, bombings, and kidnappings. But while the paramilitaries of the Weimar period had millions of members and exerted enormous influence, the RAF was tiny and comparatively marginal. Both were equally disloyal to democracy, but one posed a much bigger threat than the other.

Extremist political parties are another type of disloyal opposition. These are parties that oppose democracy as a regime type and often advocate violence, while still participating in democratic elections. As with armed groups, some are more influential than others. At one extreme, again, is Weimar Germany. The Nazi Party was the quintessential disloyal actor: it was openly hostile to the country's democracy and sought to replace it with a new regime based on what it called the "leader principle," in which Hitler would have absolute power. Many Germans were drawn to this vision, giving the Nazis back-to-back electoral victories in 1932. Other European countries saw the emergence of comparable parties during these years. The United Kingdom, for example, had the British Union of Fascists, which sought to recreate the examples of fascist Italy and Nazi Germany. It was a hateful, thuggish, thoroughly anti-democratic party. Unlike the Nazis, however, it had little popular support and never came anywhere near power.

The semi-loyal opposition is a more slippery category. These are actors who do not actively seek to overthrow democracy, but whose support for it is not absolute either. Under the right conditions, they may be willing to turn a blind eye to—or even support—an undemocratic power grab. The semi-loyal opposition is particularly important when it comes to democratic breakdown at the hands of extremist parties. Hitler's rise to power was made possible by multiple opportunistic politicians who thought they would be able to control him from the sidelines. They were wrong. Their biggest sin, however, was not their failure to appreciate Hitler's ruthlessness and cunning. It was their willingness to work with such a blatantly undemocratic figure in the first place. People loyal to democracy do not make deals with Nazis.

How can we identify the disloyal and semi-loyal opposition before it is too late? In their 2018 book *How Democracies Die*, the political scientists Steven Levitsky and Daniel Ziblatt argue that there are certain tell-tale signs of disloyalty. If politicians reject the democratic rules of the game—for example, by saying they will not accept the results of an election unless they win—that is a red flag. If they baselessly deny the legitimacy of their opponents, that is a red flag. If they tolerate or encourage violence, that is a red flag. If they indicate a willingness to curb civil liberties such as freedom of the press, that is a red flag. Semi-loyalty can be identified by looking at how actors respond to the kinds of behavior laid out in Levitsky and Ziblatt's "litmus test": do they stand pat, or do they call it out? The latter can be hard to do, especially when the disloyal behavior comes from one's own side. Being part of the loyal opposition, however, means putting the survival of democracy above one's partisan interests.

Democracy breaks down when the disloyal opposition moves from the margins to center stage, and the semi-loyal opposition lets it happen. The question, then, is why in some places, at some times, the disloyal and semi-loyal opposition overtake the loyal opposition. There are many possible contributing factors. Economic crisis, for example, can bleed support for democracy. It is no coincidence that the Nazis' rise to power occurred against the backdrop of the Great Depression of the 1930s. Another potential factor is ethnic divisions and prejudices, which can provide an opportunity for unscrupulous politicians to win power by appealing to people's worst instincts. But perhaps the biggest boost to the disloyal and semi-loyal opposition comes from the interrelated factors of polarization and fear.

Polarization and fear

It is not easy to put oneself in the shoes of someone with a radically different worldview. Most readers of this book are likely to view democracy as a desirable form of government and one worth defending. But not everybody does. Sometimes large numbers of people vote for patently disloyal parties. The Nazis came to power in Germany after winning approximately one-third of the vote in 1932—far more than any other party. Other times citizens "knock on the barracks door," or call on the military to carry out a coup. While the 1973 coup in Chile put an end to what was widely considered to be Latin America's most stable democracy, many Chileans supported it. In fact, three weeks before it happened, the lower house of Congress issued a resolution condemning Allende's government as unconstitutional, thereby "all but inviting a military coup," in the words of one prominent scholar.

Why would democratically elected congresspeople call for a coup? Why would ordinary voters cast their ballots for a party like the Nazis? While every democratic breakdown has many moving parts, a major one is nearly always polarization. The metaphor of polarization suggests a society that is pulling apart, just like the magnetic north and south poles of the Earth pull in opposite directions. Taken to its logical extreme, polarization means the division of society into two big, mutually antagonistic camps. It is particularly dangerous when it takes the form of what is known as "affective polarization." This refers to how much affection—or lack thereof—groups such as political parties feel for one another. In healthy democracies, parties disagree on important issues, but they do not hate each other. There is a high degree of what Levitsky and Ziblatt call "mutual toleration." As polarization worsens, however, this ceases to be the case. Rivals become enemies. Mutual toleration gives way to mutual hostility. Those in the other camp come to be seen not just as misguided but as treasonous. Sometimes hatred of the other side reaches such intensity that it becomes people's primary political identity—a phenomenon known as "negative partisanship." In other words, you may not love Party A, but you despise Party B.

Polarization can contribute to democratic breakdown by raising the stakes of politics to dangerous levels. If you believe the other side poses a catastrophic threat to your way of life, you may be willing to support undemocratic actions to stop them. To prevent the other side from taking power, you may cast your vote for an extremist party that promises to deliver salvation. If the other side has already come to power, you may tolerate a coup to remove them. The flipside is also true: if *your* side is in power and begins to act undemocratically, you may decide to go along with it. In principle, you may not like the idea of packing the courts, silencing the media, and locking up dissidents. But if the only alternative is to join forces with the other side—a side that you believe is beyond the pale—you may conclude that this is a price worth paying. In the context of extreme polarization, authoritarianism can seem like the lesser evil.

What underlies polarization? Sometimes it has to do with ideology: the left becomes more left-wing, the right becomes more right-wing, and the center fades into irrelevance. Other times it is rooted in identities such as race or religion, with different groups coming to see one another not as fellow citizens but as a dangerous "other." Whatever the specific form it takes, at the heart of polarization is nearly always that most primal of emotions: fear. This is not to say that such fear is justified. In fact, the flames of fear—fear of communism, fear of disorder, fear of people who look different—are often deliberately fanned by the disloyal opposition. They create the problem and then present themselves as the solution. Yet as cynical as this strategy might be, it can also be effective: when people are afraid, they may be willing to do things that they otherwise would not—even if it means voting for a Hitler or supporting a Pinochet.

The role of polarization and fear in the breakdown of democracy in Germany in the 1930s and Chile in the 1970s is hinted at by the fact that both occurred in the aftermath of two high-profile communist revolutions: the Russian Revolution of 1917 and the Cuban Revolution of 1959. Both events captured the imaginations of people around the world, with many believing it was just a matter of time before similar revolutions happened in their own countries. In Germany, this was actually attempted in 1919 during an event known as the Spartacist Uprising. Led by communists like Rosa Luxemburg and supported by thousands of striking workers, it sought to carry out a revolutionary transformation of Germany. The uprising failed, but the Communist Party of Germany, or KPD, remained a powerful force throughout the Weimar period. It had hundreds of thousands of members, boasted a massive paramilitary organization, and was a significant electoral force, often coming in third place.

Between the end of the First World War, when democracy was established in Germany, and 1933, when it died at the hands of the Nazis, the country grew increasingly polarized. This could be seen in the decline of a group of pro-democratic parties known as the "Weimar Coalition" and the simultaneous rise of extremist parties. The most important extremist parties were the far-right Nazis and the far-left KPD, whose paramilitary wings regularly fought violent street battles against each other. Both belonged to the disloyal opposition: they participated in elections as a means of reaching power, but neither was really committed to democracy as a regime type. They grew increasingly popular with German voters. In the 1928 parliamentary election, the combined vote share of the Nazis and the KPD was just 13 percent. By July 1932—the second-to-last parliamentary election before the collapse of democracy—it had skyrocketed to 51 percent.

Yet if the breakdown of democracy in Germany is a story of polarization, it is also a story of fear. The main beneficiary of this polarization—the Nazis—initially made anti-communism central to their appeal. As the political scientist Kurt Weyland has detailed, with the onset of the Great Depression and the steady rise of the KPD, many Germans feared that a communist takeover was imminent and came to see the Nazis as potential saviors. In *Mein Kampf*, Hitler called for "the elimination of the Marxist poison from our national body," claiming that communism was part of a global Jewish conspiracy. Over time, this message not only attracted growing numbers of voters, but also caused previously skeptical politicians from the semi-loyal opposition to open the doors of government to Hitler. When democracy finally died, the main trigger was an alleged communist plot: the 1933 arson attack on the country's parliament, or Reichstag. To this day, we do not know exactly how the Reichstag fire started. The Nazis, however, blamed communists, and used this as a pretext to suspend civil liberties, launch a violent crackdown on leftists, and within months to fully dismantle Germany's democracy.

Polarization and fear played a similar role in the breakdown of democracy in Chile. The Cuban Revolution of 1959 had a powerful effect on Latin America, inspiring and terrifying people in equal measure. Armed guerrilla groups sprang up throughout the region to emulate the example of revolutionaries like Fidel Castro and Ernesto "Che" Guevara. In Chile, this took the form of the Movement of the Revolutionary Left, or MIR, an armed group that sought to carry out a Cuban-style revolution. Even more significant was the effect it had on the Socialist Party, the party of Salvador Allende. While historically it had been fairly moderate, the party began to radicalize in the 1960s. At their 1967 party congress, the Socialists declared that "peaceful or legal forms of struggle...do not lead by themselves to power. The Socialist Party considers them to be limited instruments of action, incorporated into the political process that carries us to armed struggle." Allende himself was a committed democrat who believed that a revolutionary transformation of the economy could be carried out while respecting Chile's constitution. However, he was also a close

6. Chile's presidential palace during the 1973 coup.

friend of Fidel Castro and was tolerant of the MIR—in part, perhaps, because one of its main leaders was his nephew.

After Allende became president in 1970, Chile grew increasingly polarized. While the country's party system had traditionally had a strong left, a strong center, and a strong right—a three-way divide that allowed Allende to win the presidency in the first place, with just 37 percent of the vote—it soon took on a simpler dynamic: pro-Allende vs. anti-Allende. The two sides demonized each other, with Chile becoming, to quote the title of one book, a "nation of enemies." The pro-Allende side blasted the opposition for trying to block the president from carrying out his democratic mandate for radical economic change. The anti-Allende side, in turn, accused the president and his allies of trying to convert Chile into a "second Cuba." The only solution, many concluded, was for the military to intervene. Among those who agreed were the Christian Democrats, the country's most important centrist party and previously a firm defender of democracy. As polarization worsened, the Christian Democrats moved from loyal to semi-loyal opposition, throwing their support to the coup when it finally came on September 11, 1973. Many ordinary Chileans felt the same way, greeting the coup with relief or even elation.

Facing up to the challenge

The idea that something as terrible as Nazism or military rule could take power with the support of much of the population is unsettling. What lessons can be learned from past cases of democratic breakdown? One is to take the disloyal opposition seriously. These groups exist in all democracies and cannot simply be wished away. In the case of armed groups, the solution is clear: they must not be tolerated. There is no room for the violent pursuit of power in a democracy. Extremist parties pose a more difficult challenge. One option is to ban them. This is the approach that post-war Germany took to both far-right and far-left parties. The problem, of course, is that banning undemocratic parties is itself undemocratic. Another option is to establish an informal "cordon sanitaire," in which mainstream parties agree not to work with extremist parties. Many European countries have done this in recent decades, but this strategy has its own shortcomings: it can allow extremist parties to present themselves as martyrs and, in so doing, to increase their appeal among disaffected voters. How to deal with the disloyal opposition is one of democracy's knottiest dilemmas. There are no simple solutions.

The second lesson is not to dismiss the concerns of the semi-loyal opposition. These ambivalent supporters of democracy are always present—and, in many cases, their concerns are valid. A useful starting point for dealing with the challenge they pose is to distinguish between what the economist and philosopher Amartya Sen calls the "intrinsic" and "instrumental" values of democracy. The former means valuing democracy for its own sake. The latter means valuing democracy because it delivers things that people want, like "peace, order, and good government," to borrow a phrase from Canada's constitution. The semi-loyal opposition's support for democracy is instrumental. This means that if democracy fails to deliver, they may turn against it. Democratic governments must therefore do everything in their power to make sure that democracy actually works. Ideally, this would mean implementing policies that meet the needs of the many. At the very least, it means not governing so incompetently, or dismissing the preferences of the losing side of the last election so absolutely, that people stop caring whether democracy lives or dies.

Chapter 4
The life of authoritarian regimes

It is not easy to study authoritarian regimes. They tend to be hostile towards independent journalists and researchers, and their propaganda presents a highly distorted view of reality. This was a problem that Western policymakers faced during the Cold War. The Soviet Union was an extremely repressive regime with no independent media, making it very difficult to know what was really going on inside the country. This did not stop people from trying. A new discipline called "Kremlinology" emerged (in reference to the Kremlin, the country's most important government building). Kremlinologists attempted to divine who was up and who was down in the secretive world of Soviet politics by looking at things such as where officials were seated during public ceremonies and how they were described in official communications. This was more tea leaf reading than political science, but there was no alternative.

Making things even more complicated is the fact that the rules of authoritarian regimes are often unwritten. Political scientists distinguish between formal institutions, or the official rules of the game as written in constitutions and laws, and informal institutions, or rules that everybody knows but which are not to be found in any lawbook. Authoritarian regimes are dominated by informal institutions. Even basic questions like "Who is in charge?" sometimes cannot be answered by looking at formal institutions alone. In 2008, for example, President Vladimir Putin of Russia ostensibly stepped down for one term in favor of an ally, Dmitry Medvedev. Medvedev became the new president, and Putin his prime minister. This was a fiction: Putin remained in charge. When it comes to more subtle issues, like how decisions are reached in the Politburo, which kinds of corruption are tolerated and which are not, and the precise mechanics of how elections are stolen, formal institutions tell us even less.

Despite these difficulties, political scientists have made substantial progress in the study of authoritarian regimes. We now have a much better understanding of issues such as why many authoritarian regimes adopt the outward trappings of democracy, as discussed in Chapter 2. We also have a fuller appreciation of the challenges they face. The simple fact of not being a democracy turns out to yield a number of recurring problems, whether a regime is military, single-party, or personalist. This chapter examines four such problems: the problem of legitimacy, the problem of information, the problem of frenemies, and the problem of succession. While some authoritarian regimes have managed to find workarounds to these problems, they are largely intractable. They are part of the authoritarian condition, and are simply not present in democracies to the same degree.

Problem of legitimacy

The concept of legitimacy lies at the heart of all political regimes. Legitimacy is the answer to a moral question: "What right do you have to rule?" In democracies, the answer is simple: "Because the people elected us." It is more difficult for authoritarian regimes. The idea that such regimes would even try to legitimate themselves may come as a surprise to some readers. Why not simply bludgeon the population into submission? To be sure, all authoritarian regimes use coercion, ranging from threats against journalists to full-blown massacres. Extreme repression can backfire, however, with a desperate population concluding, to quote the title of one book, that there is "no other way out" than to take up arms. Over-reliance on the secret police and other security agencies can also lead to these agencies becoming rival power centers and thus a threat to the regime's top leaders. Finally, there is a more mundane consideration: large-scale repression is expensive and logistically complicated. It is simpler and cheaper to make people want to obey than to have them do so out of fear alone.

What, then, can authoritarian regimes do to legitimate themselves? Three possible sources of legitimacy are the divine right of kings, communist ideology, and religion. Each, however, has obvious limitations: they apply only to monarchies, communist regimes, and theocracies, respectively. Many authoritarian regimes rely instead on what the political scientist Samuel P. Huntington called "negative legitimacy" and "performance legitimacy." Negative legitimacy refers not to what a regime is *for* but what it is *against*. It is based on what he calls the "anti" appeals: anti-communism, anti-chaos, and so forth. Where authoritarian rule was preceded by a high degree of polarization, these appeals may resonate with much of the population. Negative legitimacy, however, has a paradoxical effect: the better an authoritarian regime is at protecting against the perceived threat, the more distant the memory of that threat becomes and the less likely it is to generate ongoing support. The regime becomes a victim of its own success.

The declining potency of negative legitimacy leads many authoritarian regimes to the second option: performance legitimacy. Here the regime claims a right to rule based on its ability to produce things that people value, such as economic prosperity or national glory. Some authoritarian regimes have overseen economic miracles, such as Taiwan's single-party regime (1949–2000) and South Korea's military regime (1961–87). In little more than a generation, both went from grinding poverty to fully developed status. However, hitching a regime's legitimacy to its economic performance has drawbacks. First, most authoritarian regimes do *not* manage the economy well. The cases of Taiwan and South Korea are so interesting precisely because they are so unusual. Second, even if they do manage the economy well, they are still subject to the ups and downs of the business cycle and to international shocks, with potentially fatal consequences. Indonesia's New Order regime (1966–98) oversaw decades of economic growth, but then collapsed in the wake of the Asian Financial Crisis of 1997. It is risky to stake a regime's legitimacy on factors that it does not fully control.

Another option for performance legitimacy is nationalism. Here the regime tries to harness people's love of country by promising to make the nation great again. This, too, is risky. If an authoritarian regime launches a military adventure in pursuit of national glory, and then loses, the population may turn against it. A good example is Argentina. During its last period of military rule (1976–83), the country's rulers decided to invade the Falkland Islands, a sparsely populated British overseas territory off the coast of South America that Argentina has long claimed as its own (it calls them the Malvinas). The goal was to win support for the regime in the midst of a worsening economic crisis—and it worked. The invasion was extremely popular with Argentines, even among leftists who had been violently persecuted by the military regime. This "rally 'round the flag" effect proved short-lived, however. The United Kingdom sent warships to defend the islands, and the Argentine military quickly surrendered. Nationalist fervor gave way to national humiliation, and support for Argentina's military regime curdled into rage. A little over a year later, the country returned to democracy.

Problem of information

If authoritarian regimes wish to be seen as legitimate, it follows that they must also wish to know something about public opinion.

What are people thinking? What are their grievances? Do they support the regime or oppose it? For democracies, it is easy to answer such questions. They can simply commission a poll—which they do, frequently. This information is much harder to access under authoritarianism, for a simple reason: people have a strong incentive to lie. If you live in Stalinist Russia and are asked whether you support Stalin, the obvious answer is "yes." If perceived dissidence can lead to imprisonment or death, it is in your interests to smile and nod. The political scientist Timur Kuran calls this "preference falsification." It is rife in authoritarian regimes. The more repressive the regime, the worse it is likely to be. This can make authoritarian regimes appear more stable than they really are. The masses may be outwardly supportive, but underneath they are seething. If some unforeseen event suddenly makes the regime appear vulnerable, they may rise up against it without warning. This is the stuff of nightmares for autocrats.

The incentive to lie applies not just to the public, but also to authoritarian officials. Autocrats do not like to hear the word "no." Even less do they like to be told that their ideas are infeasible, immoral, or insane. Those who dare to voice such opinions are likely to be replaced by sycophants. The result has been described as the "dictator trap": as the autocrat surrounds himself with people who tell him whatever he wants to hear, he ceases to get good advice and eventually makes a major policy blunder. One example is Putin in Russia, who during his decades in power came to inhabit an information bubble that bore little resemblance to reality. In 2022, Putin made the fateful decision to invade Ukraine—apparently on the belief that the Ukrainians would not put up much of a fight, and that Ukraine was not a real country anyway. He was wrong on both counts. The result was massive economic sanctions, hundreds of thousands of Russian casualties, and a military quagmire. As one senior advisor to Ukraine's president commented on Twitter in October 2022 after Ukrainian troops retook a city under Russian control: "Reality can hurt if you live in a fantasy world."

What, if anything, can authoritarian regimes do to solve the problem of information? There are various tools for gauging public opinion, though all have shortcomings. Elections are one option. As discussed in earlier chapters, many authoritarian regimes today feel compelled to hold multi-party elections due to international pressure and the global spread of democratic ideas. However, elections have an added advantage: they can tell autocrats where they have support, where they are opposed, and where there has been change over time. Armed with this information, they can then respond either by punishing places that failed to vote in the "correct" way or by directing resources to those places in an effort to win back support. Elections, however, pose a dilemma: on the one hand, to be a source of accurate information, they must be at least somewhat competitive. On the other hand, allowing competitive elections can open a Pandora's box that puts the regime's survival at risk, as we shall see in Chapter 5 in the case of Chile.

Authoritarian regimes that do not hold multi-party elections must rely on other methods to learn about the public's mood. As the political scientist Martin K. Dimitrov has documented, some communist regimes during the Cold War employed a surprising tool: they actively encouraged citizens to complain. By calling for formal complaints about shortages of goods, poor public services, and other issues of daily concern, they sought to learn about the public's grievances so that they could devise solutions before it was too late. There was a lot to complain about, and people responded to the call. In communist Bulgaria, one out of every 10 adults contacted the authorities with a grievance in 1984 alone. This amounted to a kind of "barometer of public opinion," in the words of the Bulgarian Communist Party. This barometer, however, did not answer the most important question of all: did people really support the regime, or were they just pretending and waiting for a moment of weakness? While citizens might be willing to complain about bread-and-butter issues, most knew better than to reveal their preferences about communist rule itself. In 1989, when mass uprisings broke out and toppled communist regimes throughout Eastern Europe, they took everyone by surprise—not least the communist authorities themselves.

Problem of frenemies

A third challenge for authoritarian regimes is to remain united. While such regimes try to present an image of cohesion to the outside world, in truth they are always divided into different groups or factions—factions that often dislike each other. They might work together, but they are not friends. They are "frenemies," to use a term coined over a century ago that has come into vogue in recent years. One potential source of division is ideology, with disagreements over whether, for example, to have a fully planned economy or to allow some market activity. Another is pure ambition, with different groups of officials clustering around rival "big men" in the hope of riding their coat-tails to the top. Finally, there is the division between what political scientists call "hardliners" and "softliners." These are groups who disagree on whether the regime should stick to its guns and simply beat back the opposition, or try to placate it through policies such as relaxing censorship, releasing political prisoners, and holding elections for some offices. Hardliners say, "we will not give an inch." Softliners say, "something's gotta give."

The problem of frenemies, of course, is not confined to authoritarian regimes. Democracies also have their fair share of infighting. One example is Australia, which between 2010 and 2018 saw its prime minister overthrown by rival factions in his or her own party a whopping four times. The same fate befell Margaret Thatcher in the United Kingdom: in 1990, after 11 years in office, she was forced to resign by her own Conservative Party and replaced as prime minister by one of her cabinet ministers, John Major. Yet as dramatic as these "leadership spills" were, they did not imperil democracy. Prime ministers rose and fell, but no blood was shed. More common still is for factional rivalries to be settled through party primaries or leadership contests. These can get heated, as with the 2016 Democratic Party's presidential primary in the United States pitting centrist Hillary Clinton against democratic socialist Bernie Sanders. Such contests, however, are a routine part of democratic politics.

The stakes are much higher under authoritarianism. For the person at the top, there is always the threat of a palace coup. Even worse is a bullet in the head. In South Korea, long-time military ruler Park Chung-hee was assassinated by the chief of his secret police in 1979. The military ruler of Bangladesh, Ziaur Rahman, was assassinated by rival army officers in 1981. The communist ruler of Romania, Nicolae Ceaușescu, was summarily executed by the military in 1989. The threats of overthrow or assassination can lead to paranoia on the part of autocrats—and from there to terror against their own officials. One example is the Night of the Long Knives in Germany. In 1934, Hitler ordered the execution of scores of Nazi officials whom he viewed as potential threats. The most high-profile victim was Ernst Röhm, the head of the Nazis' powerful paramilitary wing, the SA, and one of Hitler's closest friends. Communist regimes in the Soviet Union and China carried out even more extensive purges of their own ranks.

This surprising aspect of authoritarian regimes—that despite exerting control over the population, their officials must live in constant fear of one another—has been well explored in fiction. A prominent example is George Orwell's *Nineteen Eighty-Four*, which introduced the world to terms like "Big Brother" and the "Thought Police." It tells the story of Winston Smith, an apparently ordinary person living under the most all-controlling regime ever conceived. He is eventually arrested, tortured, and killed. In one way, however, Smith is *not* ordinary. He works at the propaganda ministry and is a member of "the Party," whose members, Orwell tells us, make up only 15 percent of the population. In other words, he is a regime official, albeit a low-level one. The bulk of the population—the "proles," as the novel calls them—live in relative freedom compared to Party members like Smith. This theme of authoritarian regimes terrorizing their own officials is also explored in Arthur Koestler's classic novel *Darkness at Noon* (1940) about a purged high-level official in an unnamed communist regime, as well as in the Latin American genre of fiction known as the "dictator novel."

The problem of frenemies can not only make life terrifying for authoritarian officials but can also threaten the survival of the regime itself. This idea was famously captured by the political scientists Guillermo O'Donnell and Philippe Schmitter in an important 1986 book, when they wrote: "[T]here is no transition whose beginning is not the consequence—direct or indirect—of important divisions within the authoritarian regime itself, principally along the fluctuating cleavage between hard-liners and soft-liners." This is probably an exaggeration. Foreign military occupation, for example, can also lead to regime change, as it did in Japan and Germany after the Second World War. Nevertheless, there is little doubt that factional splits or "schisms" can be perilous for authoritarian regimes. The reason is simple: in a fight between banners and machine guns, the machine guns will always win. If authoritarian officials decide to hang together and use whatever means necessary to cling to power, there is not much the opposition can do. However, if those officials split over how best to respond to challenges such as mass protests, foreign pressure, or economic crisis, this can create an opening for the opposition and trigger the downfall of the regime.

What, if anything, can authoritarian regimes do to prevent schisms? Political parties can help. When an official ruling party exists, the dividing line between insiders and outsiders is clear: those who join the party are insiders, and those who do not are outsiders. If access to power and influence—not to mention the ill-gotten gains of corruption—requires party membership, there is a strong incentive to stick with the party. In political science jargon, parties lengthen people's "time horizons": they make their members think not just about immediate gains and losses, but about their longer-term interests. If you belong to a faction that loses a fight over a prized policy or plum position, you may be unhappy about it—but you will not abandon the regime and join the opposition. You lost this round, but you're still a regime insider and can hope to win the next one.

The role of parties in preventing schisms helps to explain a striking pattern among authoritarian regimes: single-party regimes tend to last longer than military or personalist regimes. In a study of authoritarian regimes from 1946 to 1998, the political scientist Barbara Geddes found that while military regimes lasted for an average of nine years and personalist regimes for 15 years, single-party regimes lasted for 23 years. Yet as useful as ruling parties are for holding authoritarian regimes together, they are not a magic bullet. Few single-party regimes last anywhere near as long as the Soviet Union (69 years), the PRI regime in Mexico (71 years), or communist China (75 years and counting). Even in regimes that do, this will come as cold comfort to those officials executed or imprisoned on the paranoid whims of the dominant faction.

Problem of succession

Finally, authoritarian regimes face the problem of succession. Who replaces the leader when he dies or is incapacitated? This is not a problem in democracies, since the rules of succession are usually clear. A president who dies in office is typically replaced by the vice president, as occurred in the United States after the 1963 assassination of President John F. Kennedy. When a prime minister dies, the governing party simply chooses a new leader, as the Congress Party did in India following the death of Prime Minister Jawaharlal Nehru in 1964. The death and replacement of a head of government is a big event, but it does not put democracy at risk. Even the issue of earning a mandate can easily be solved by holding new elections. Whether special elections are convened or the normal electoral clock is allowed to play out, sooner or later the new leader will have to face the verdict of the electorate, as Kennedy's vice president and successor, Lyndon B. Johnson, did in 1964. He won a landslide victory—far in excess, in fact, of what Kennedy had earned four years earlier.

The problem of succession is much more serious for authoritarian regimes. In the most extreme cases, the death of the leader can trigger a regime transition. The most famous example is Franco in Spain. In 1975, after three and a half decades in power, the 82-year-old leader died of natural causes—and, almost immediately, the country began to democratize. This is actually quite a rare outcome, as the political scientists Andrea Kendall-Taylor and Erica Frantz have shown. But even if the death or retirement of the leader does not usually trigger a regime transition, things can still get ugly quickly. This ugliness is mined for dramatic purposes in the popular HBO television show *Succession*, which tells the fictional story of an ailing corporate boss, Logan Roy, and the struggle among his adult children over who should succeed him as head of the family business. The dynamics in authoritarian regimes are similar, but with much higher stakes. The death of Joseph Stalin in 1953 and Mao Zedong in 1976 led to ferocious power struggles in the Soviet Union and China, respectively, with punishments for the losers ranging from banishments to remote areas to death sentences.

What, if anything, can authoritarian regimes do to address the problem of succession? Many simply put off the issue for as long as possible. In Cuba, Fidel Castro remained in power for 49 years, only stepping down as president in 2008 at the age of 81. He then handed power to his brother, Raúl, who stepped down in 2018 at the age of 86. In Zimbabwe, Robert Mugabe ruled from 1980 until 2017, before finally being overthrown by the military at the age of 93. To make explicit their long-term claims to power, some autocrats will literally declare themselves "President for Life," as independence leaders Kwame Nkrumah of Ghana and Sukarno of

7. Cuba's Fidel Castro with brother and successor Raúl.

Indonesia did in the 1960s. (This proved to be overly optimistic; both were overthrown by the military not long after.) Even more collective forms of rule can see top officials cling to power until deep into old age. In 1980, the average age of a Politburo member in the Soviet Union was 70—at a time when life expectancy in the country was 68 years. This has earned some authoritarian regimes the moniker of "gerontocracy," or rule of the old.

Eventually, though, the issue of succession must be faced. No ruler is immortal. The solution chosen by many authoritarian regimes is the dynastic principle: the son replaces the father. While this is not surprising in the context of personalist regimes, it also happens in other kinds of authoritarian regime. Two examples are Taiwan and Singapore, single-party regimes whose competent economic management made them into "Asian Tigers." These regimes took governance seriously. Nevertheless, following the death of long-time Taiwanese leader Chiang Kai-shek in 1975 and the retirement of Singaporean leader Lee Kuan Yew in 2004, both regimes opted to replace these leaders with their first-born sons. Why? In his study of hereditary succession in modern autocracies, the political scientist Jason Brownlee argues that this can serve as the least bad option for authoritarian officials. While each official would like to become the new ruler himself, they all fear the consequences of a power struggle. To minimize this risk, they decide to back the former autocrat's son as a consensus candidate.

A much rarer solution is for authoritarian regimes to develop more predictable or "institutionalized" rules for succession. The best example is Mexico under the PRI. During its seven decades of hegemonic-party rule, the PRI held regular presidential elections and always won. The new president would then exercise absolute power for six years—but with a strictly enforced one-term limit. In the lead-up to the next election, the outgoing president would choose a successor from his cabinet, who would then repeat the process. This was known as the "*dedazo*," stemming from the Spanish word for finger (since the outgoing president essentially pointed to his replacement). It was a purely informal institution: it was not written down anywhere, but it was studiously followed for decades. This case was exceptional, however. The difficulty of institutionalizing succession in authoritarian regimes is well illustrated by communist China, which, beginning in the 1990s, seemed to be moving toward something like the *dedazo*. A new rule emerged that the regime's top leader would serve two five-year terms, and then step down. However, after Xi Jinping came to power in 2012, he abandoned this rule, engineering a third term for himself and potentially setting the stage to become president for life.

Chapter 5
The death of authoritarian regimes

Why do authoritarian regimes die? One answer that has long guided Western policymakers is economic development. While the term "political science" is more aspiration than reality, if it has one finding that comes close to being a scientific fact, it is this: development and democracy tend to go hand in hand. This idea was famously captured by the sociologist and political scientist Seymour Martin Lipset, who asserted in a 1959 article that "the more well-to-do a nation, the greater the chances that it will sustain democracy." This became the bedrock of what is known as modernization theory—and it has stood up remarkably well over time. Nearly all of the richest countries in the world in per capita income are democratic, while nearly all of the poorest are authoritarian. (The main exceptions are the oil-rich authoritarian regimes known as "petrostates," which, as discussed in Chapter 6, possess some unique characteristics.)

There are several reasons why economic development might make democracy more likely. One is education. As people learn to read and write and gain more knowledge about public affairs, they become less willing to be ruled. They want to have a say. Another is the growth of the middle class. While the wealthy few tend to be content with the status quo, this growing class of people with some means—the lawyers and doctors and shopkeepers and teachers—would like to see power more widely distributed.

In particular, they would like to see it distributed to themselves. Finally, development triggers the emergence of new organized groups that cannot be easily crushed. As people move from the countryside to the city, and from the farm to the factory, they meet more and more people with interests similar to their own. The voluntary groups that they form, from Bible-reading clubs to NGOs, are collectively known as "civil society." Of particular importance are labor unions, whose mass memberships and high levels of organization have often given them a leading role in the struggle against authoritarianism.

Yet while modernization theory has earned its place as one of the most influential theories of political regimes and regime transitions, it does not tell the whole story. There are a good number of poor democracies in the world—most notably India, which has been democratic for most of the period since its independence in 1947 (though its democracy came under assault after the election of Narendra Modi as prime minister in 2014, as noted in Chapter 2). Modernization theory also tells us little about the specific triggers of democratization. It is the quintessential example of a "structural" theory: it emphasizes deeply rooted, slow-moving changes to a country's economy and society. Transitions to democracy, however, often happen quickly and are triggered by identifiable events. Two possible triggers are the death of the autocrat and loss in war, as discussed in Chapter 4. An even more common trigger is economic crisis. For example, many Latin American countries in the 1980s were rocked by what became known as the "debt crisis." As economies shrank and inflation soared, authoritarian regimes lost legitimacy. Within a couple of decades, Latin America went from being a region that was mostly authoritarian to one that was mostly democratic.

This chapter discusses two factors that can contribute to the death of authoritarian regimes and their replacement by democracy: changes in the international environment and leadership. As we saw in Chapter 3, the Russian Revolution of 1917 and the Cuban Revolution of 1959 sent shock waves through Europe and Latin

America, directly contributing to the breakdown of democracy in countries like Germany and Chile. However, in the final decades of the 20th century, changes in the United States, the Soviet Union, and the Catholic Church had the opposite effect: they made the world much less hospitable to authoritarianism. These changes in the international environment put pressure on authoritarian regimes to relinquish power. The leadership of people like South Africa's Nelson Mandela, in turn, helped to allay the fears of authoritarian officials and their supporters, thus making a transition to democracy more likely.

International environment

"No man is an island, entire of itself," wrote the 17th-century English poet John Donne; "every man is a piece of the continent, a part of the main." The same is true of countries. They do not exist in isolation, but instead are affected by their neighbors, faraway superpowers, and other international factors. Sometimes these factors align in a broadly pro-democratic direction; other times they favor authoritarianism. The defeat of the Axis powers in 1945 seemed, briefly, to usher in a world more conducive to democracy. The Allies had framed the Second World War as a struggle for freedom, and they successfully managed to impose democracy in Japan and West Germany. However, the very fact that Germany was divided into two—the capitalist West, and the communist East—was a sign of problems to come. Despite being allies during the war, relations between the United States and the Soviet Union quickly soured. As they settled into a new Cold War, democracy became one of its casualties. The Soviet Union was explicitly hostile to democracy, using force to prop up communist regimes in Eastern Europe. The U.S., in turn, often threw its support to repressive anti-communist regimes, on the principle of "the enemy of my enemy is my friend."

Eventually, however, the international environment began to shift back in a more pro-democratic direction. This was one of the main factors highlighted by Samuel P. Huntington to explain the third wave of democratization, as discussed in Chapter 1. One major change occurred within the Catholic Church. Historically, the church had been lukewarm about democracy. It endorsed a principle known as "error has no rights," which called for the state to suppress the public expression of non-Catholic faiths, and it often cozied up to right-wing autocrats like Franco in Spain. In 1962–5, however, the church underwent a process of introspection known as the Second Vatican Council, or Vatican II. This led to reforms such as holding Mass in the language of local congregants rather than Latin—and also, crucially, to greater support for democracy and human rights. By the 1970s and 1980s, church leaders had become leading actors in the struggle against authoritarianism in countries such as Brazil, Chile, and the Philippines. Indeed, the first phase of the third wave was so dominated by Catholic-majority countries that it has been dubbed the "Catholic wave."

One country where the Catholic Church played an especially important role was Poland. Like other countries in Eastern

8. **Solidarity banner in Poland depicting Pope John Paul II.**

Europe, Soviet occupation after the Second World War led to communist rule. Unusually for a communist country, however, the church was granted a high degree of autonomy, a concession to Poland's tradition of devout Catholicism. A major turning point came in 1978 when Karol Wojtyła, the archbishop of Kraków, became Pope John Paul II. In 1979, he visited his native country and gave a series of speeches before mass audiences in which he mixed religious teachings with criticism of Poland's communist regime. One year later, a new organization called Solidarity emerged—technically a labor union, but in reality a mass-based social movement dedicated to the overthrow of communism. By 1981, Solidarity had approximately 10 million members (in a country of 36 million people). After a decade of struggle, communism fell and Poland democratized. By all accounts, the pope's contribution was critical. As the country's president put it after the death of John Paul II in 2005: "We wouldn't have had a free Poland without him."

The second change in the international environment was in U.S. foreign policy. During the presidency of Richard Nixon (1969–74), the United States was guided by "realpolitik"—a philosophy that holds, in effect, that anything goes if it is believed to be in the national interest. This sometimes led to blatantly anti-democratic behavior. One notorious example was the 1973 overthrow of Salvador Allende in Chile. As discussed in Chapter 3, the election of a leftist president was a terrifying prospect for many Chileans. The U.S. government took a similarly bleak view, fearing that Allende would inspire leftists in other countries. To prevent this from happening, multiple U.S. agencies conspired, first, to prevent Allende from taking office, and then, when that failed, to encourage a coup against him. While U.S. interference was not the only factor behind the coup, at the very least it made a bad situation worse and became a symbol of the United States' abandonment of democracy during the Cold War.

Soon, however, the U.S. began to reverse course. During the presidency of Jimmy Carter (1977–81), a progressive evangelical Christian, the U.S. government made human rights a central plank of its foreign policy. It began to criticize and cut off military aid to authoritarian regimes that it had previously regarded as allies. This continued, albeit inconsistently, during the presidency of Ronald Reagan (1981–9)—including in Chile, whose democracy the U.S. had only recently helped to destroy. According to the military regime's constitution, a plebiscite had to be held by 1988, in which voters would be asked whether they wanted Pinochet to remain in power. In the lead-up to the plebiscite, the U.S. pressured the Chilean government to hold a relatively free and fair vote, and then provided funding to the anti-Pinochet "No" campaign. The U.S. also made clear that it would oppose any attempt to reject the results if Pinochet lost. When Pinochet tried to cling to power through violence after losing the plebiscite, he was informed by other members of the junta that he did not have their support and was forced to back down. (This episode also illustrates that in military regimes, even if one officer becomes the public face of the regime, it is the junta that has the final word.)

Finally, changes in the Soviet Union had a profound impact on the international environment. After the Second World War, the Soviet Union made clear that it would not accept challenges to communism in what it considered its own backyard. This was not an idle threat. In 1956, it invaded Hungary to put down a mass uprising against communist rule. In 1968, the Soviet Union and its allies invaded Czechoslovakia to put a stop to the "Prague Spring," where the communist authorities had begun to experiment with greater political openness. The Soviet Union started to change, however, after a new leader, Mikhail Gorbachev, came to power in 1985. He began to implement far-reaching reforms under the headings of "perestroika" (restructuring) and "glasnost" (openness). These reforms allowed for greater market activity in the Soviet economy and new political liberties for Soviet citizens, including significant room for freedom of speech.

The changes unleashed by Gorbachev helped to tilt the world in a more democratic direction in two ways. First, the Soviet Union abandoned the "Brezhnev Doctrine," through which it had claimed the right to intervene in countries like Hungary and Czechoslovakia, in favor of the so-called "Sinatra Doctrine," a joking reference to Frank Sinatra's song "My Way." Under Gorbachev, in other words, Eastern European countries were now free to do it "their way"—they could do what they wanted. What they wanted, it turned out, was not to be communist. In 1989, communist regimes fell in rapid succession throughout Eastern Europe, picking up speed as they went. As one saying put it: "In Poland, it took ten years, in Hungary ten months, in East Germany ten weeks, in Czechoslovakia ten days, and in Romania ten hours." In 1991, the Soviet Union itself collapsed, breaking up into 15 separate countries (though unlike in Eastern Europe, most of these countries became new authoritarian regimes, not democracies).

The second effect of Gorbachev's reforms was indirect. During the Cold War, the Soviet Union—or "Evil Empire," as Reagan famously called it—served as a convenient justification for right-wing authoritarian regimes. Democracy could not be permitted, they argued, as this would open the doors to communism. One example is South Africa, whose apartheid regime was not only racist but also virulently anti-communist. It portrayed itself as a lonely outpost of capitalism on the African continent. This self-portrayal was aided by the African National Congress, or ANC, the organization that led the struggle against apartheid. The ANC called for the nationalization of much of the economy, received support from the Soviet Union, and had close relations with the South African Communist Party. In fact, some of the ANC's top leaders held membership in both parties—including Nelson Mandela, who, it was later revealed, had even served on the central committee of the Communist Party. In addition, the ANC decided to abandon the non-violent tactics that it had hitherto supported in favor of armed struggle, with Mandela becoming the leader of the new armed wing of the party. The authorities responded by banning the ANC and sentencing Mandela to life imprisonment.

The rise of Gorbachev upended this communism/anti-communism dynamic. Suddenly the Soviet Union became a less scary place—and thus a less compelling foil for right-wing autocrats. It is no coincidence that apartheid began to crumble just a few months after the fall of the Berlin Wall. In February 1990, South Africa's recently minted president, F. W. de Klerk, decided to unban the ANC and release Mandela from prison. Many factors contributed to this decision, including mass resistance by South African civil society and an international campaign to divest from the country's economy. The changes unleashed by Gorbachev, however, were critical. As de Klerk later reflected in an interview: "The fall of the Berlin Wall and the breakdown of the Soviet Union as an expansionist world power that sought control over southern Africa really opened a window of opportunity. I don't think I could have included everything that I did in the package of February 2, 1990, if the Berlin Wall had not come down." For that window to open in the direction of democracy, however, it would take more than changes in the international environment. It would also take leadership.

Leadership

Political scientists do not like to talk about individual leaders. We want to develop theories to make sense of broad patterns, not explain one-off events. To say "X leader made such-and-such a decision and that is why democratization happened" is not much of a theory. Nevertheless, it is undeniable that leadership can have a major impact on transitions from authoritarian rule. To understand how, we must return to one of the core insights from Chapter 3: democratic breakdown rarely happens without some degree of popular support. When people are afraid, they may seek refuge in the disloyal opposition. The same principle applies once authoritarian rule has been established, with many backing the regime out of fear of what might happen if democratization were permitted. The political scientist Robert A. Dahl calls such considerations the "costs of toleration." Will they be killed? Will they be forced into exile? Will they lose their property? Or will nothing much at all happen? The higher the costs of toleration, the more likely authoritarian officials and their supporters are to do everything possible to prevent democratization.

Leaders of the democratic opposition can play a pivotal role in lowering the costs of toleration. One way is through what we might call the politics of grace. This is when democratic leaders, through their words and deeds, signal to the other side that they need not be afraid. Here the undisputed master was Nelson Mandela, who, after spending 27 years as a political prisoner, led South Africa's transition to democracy and became its first-ever democratically elected president in 1994. Both during and after the transition, Mandela made clear that his vision of South Africa was a broad and generous one—it should be a "Rainbow Nation," with room for people of all colors. He emphasized forgiveness rather than retribution. He learned Afrikaans, the language spoken by many white South Africans. During the 1995 Rugby World Cup, he went out of his way to support the country's nearly all-white national team. These gestures were all the more remarkable given Mandela's history as a guerrilla fighter—a history that earned him a spot on the U.S. government's terrorism watch list until 2008.

A second way that leaders can help to lower the costs of toleration is by negotiating a democratic "pact." While gestures such as Mandela's are important, sometimes a more concrete set of promises is needed to win over skeptics. Pact-making is when

9. Nelson Mandela and outgoing apartheid leader F. W. de Klerk.

authoritarian officials, leaders of the opposition, and key societal actors such as business and labor come together to negotiate an agreement about the contours of the new regime. The point of departure for pacts is that different actors have different "vital interests," as the political scientists Guillermo O'Donnell and Philippe Schmitter call them—and that it is imperative to secure those interests if democracy is to take hold. The military, for example, might believe it is vitally important that its budget not be cut. The wealthy might believe it is vitally important that their property not be expropriated. Authoritarian officials might believe it is vitally important that they not be tried for human rights abuses. Agreeing to concessions like these is not easy. It amounts, in essence, to making a deal with the devil. But it may be worth it if it helps to bring about the end of authoritarianism.

Pacts have played a key role in some of history's most celebrated cases of democratization, including the Pact of Punto Fijo in Venezuela in 1958 and the Pacts of Moncloa in Spain in 1977. The former helped Venezuela not only to become a democracy, but to remain one during the 1960s and 1970s at a time when other Latin American countries were suffering coups. The latter helped Spain to become one of the pioneers of the third wave of democratization after decades of authoritarianism and civil war. A more recent example of a "pacted" transition is South Africa. While de Klerk's decision to unban the ANC and release Mandela from prison in 1990 was an important first step, there was no guarantee that this would culminate in a peaceful transition to democracy. Even anti-apartheid activists like the South African novelist Nadine Gordimer believed that civil war was a real possibility, a scenario she depicted in her 1981 novel *July's People*. Instead, South Africa experienced three years of heated negotiations between apartheid officials and the ANC, followed by democratic elections in 1994.

The agreement reached in South Africa's negotiations essentially boiled down to this: democracy would be introduced on the principle of "one person, one vote" (a painful concession for racist supporters of apartheid), while the highly unequal, white-dominated economy would remain in place (a painful concession for leftist supporters of the ANC). On the issue of human rights, they basically agreed to split the difference. There would be no human rights trials, but neither would the past be swept under the rug. Instead, a Truth and Reconciliation Commission was created, in which abuses committed under apartheid were publicly aired in exchange for amnesty. Some on the ANC side argued that all of this amounted to a "Faustian" bargain—that too much had been given away, particularly with respect to the economy. Such critiques are often levelled against pacts. Those who favor pacts, however, believe that we should not let perfect be the enemy of good. Even a mediocre democracy, in this view, is better than something like apartheid.

A final way that leaders can have an impact is with respect to democratic consolidation. This refers not to whether democracy emerges, but to whether it becomes the "only game in town," as the political scientists Juan J. Linz and Alfred Stepan memorably put it. One way that leaders can help democracy become the only game in town is by not alienating supporters of the old regime to such a degree that they rise up against the new one. Democratic leaders can also contribute to it in a second, more surprising way: by not becoming autocrats themselves. It is sadly common for former leaders of the opposition, after being elected to office, to install their own authoritarian regimes—a process that has been described as "one man, one vote, one time." It takes a special kind of leader to resist this temptation. The most famous example is George Washington, who, after leading the United States to independence, voluntarily stepped down—not once, but twice: first as commander of the Continental Army in 1783, and then in 1797 after two serving terms as president. Upon hearing of Washington's plans to step down as head of the military, King George III of Great Britain reportedly said: "If he does that, he will be the greatest man in the world."

As with so many things, the benchmark for this kind of self-sacrificing leadership in our time was set by Nelson Mandela. In 1999, after serving a single five-year term, Mandela retired from active politics. To see how differently things might have gone with a different leader at the helm, we need only look across the border to Zimbabwe. Like South Africa, Zimbabwe (formerly Rhodesia) was an ex-British colony whose white minority established an authoritarian regime in which the country's black majority was largely excluded. This led to an armed insurgency against the regime in the 1960s and 1970s, and finally to the holding of democratic elections in 1980. The elections were won by the Zimbabwe African National Union, or ZANU, whose leader, Robert Mugabe, became prime minister (and later president). However, unlike his fellow guerrilla-leader-turned-democratically-elected-president, Nelson Mandela, Mugabe did not relinquish power. He established a new authoritarian regime and ruled for the next 37 years.

People power

Like all political outcomes, the death of authoritarian regimes—and, relatedly, the transition to democracy—is not the result of just one thing. To use the jargon of political science, regime change is "multi-causal" and "probabilistic": many factors contribute to it, none of them totally determinative. This chapter has focused on two such factors. The impact of leadership is obvious. For the good of democracy, it is better to be led by a Nelson Mandela than a Robert Mugabe. The impact of the international environment is equally clear. It is harder to maintain authoritarianism when the United States and the Catholic Church are pushing for democracy and the Soviet Union has started to loosen its grip. Changes in the international environment, in turn, do not appear out of nowhere. They are shaped by the decisions of individual leaders, whether Carter, Gorbachev, or John Paul II.

All of this should give us hope. The death of authoritarian regimes is not brought about by abstract forces alone. While structural conditions—such as level of development, or, as discussed in Chapter 6, culture—can be more or less favorable, there is always room for maneuver. Structure matters, but it is not destiny. At the end of the day, it is people who make history—and not just presidents and Nobel Prize winners. The heroic actions of ordinary people can shake the foundations of authoritarian regimes, as they did during the 1986 "People Power Revolution" in the Philippines, when millions of people took to the streets to demand the end of the 21-year reign of Ferdinand Marcos. Their demand was met: Marcos fled the country, and democracy took root. The actions of ordinary people played a key role in other democratic transitions, too. The millions of Solidarity members in Poland, civil society activists in South Africa, and voters in Chile who cast their ballots against Pinochet really did make a difference.

Even more heartening is the fact democratic activists can learn from each other. This is known as the "demonstration effect." This is when people in one country look at events in another country and take inspiration. The demonstration effect is especially strong among countries with shared geographical, linguistic, or cultural ties, and helps to explain why democratic uprisings often follow a wave-like pattern, as in Eastern Europe in 1989. The basic logic underlying the demonstration effect is: "If they can do it, why not us?" Unfortunately, this does not just apply to democrats. Autocrats can also learn from one another—one of the factors that helps to explain the puzzle of authoritarian durability, the topic of the next chapter.

Chapter 6
The puzzle of authoritarian durability

The third wave of democratization that washed over the world at the end of the 20th century left many islands of authoritarianism in place. The existence of authoritarian regimes is not mysterious in and of itself. It is democracy that has been the historical rarity, not authoritarianism. The mystery is why some authoritarian regimes have been so much more resilient than others. The best example is China. In 1989, as communist regimes began to fall like dominoes throughout Eastern Europe, it seemed like China might be next. In April of that year, mass pro-democracy protests broke out across the country. The symbolic center of the movement was Beijing's Tiananmen Square, though protests took place in hundreds of cities, with millions of participants. However, the protests ended in tragedy, not democracy. On June 4, the military opened fire, killing hundreds—possibly thousands—of unarmed civilians. The massacre put an end to China's incipient democracy movement, and it has never recovered.

Why do some authoritarian regimes survive while others die? What allows some to withstand challenges such as mass protests, economic crises, and international pressure, while the same factors bring others crashing down? This is the puzzle of authoritarian durability. One possible answer is culture. The values and beliefs of different societies shape how people work, worship, and love. It is not far-fetched to think that they could also have an impact on politics. It has been argued, for example, that Confucianism, the set of beliefs developed 2,500 years ago by the Chinese philosopher Confucius, is hostile to democracy. Confucianism, in this view, emphasizes hierarchy over equality and the group over the individual, and thus is a poor fit for the rough-and-tumble of democratic politics. This is known as the "Asian values" thesis. Similar claims have been made about Islam. Some argue, for example, that Islam does not make a clear distinction between church and state, which impedes the free flow of ideas and the ability to criticize governments that democracy requires.

As with other deeply rooted structural factors, it is probably true that some cultures provide more fertile terrain for democracy than others. However, there are good reasons to be skeptical of the strongest versions of the cultural argument. One reason is the identity of its proponents. The most high-profile proponent of the Asian values thesis was none other than Lee Kuan Yew, the long-time former autocrat of Singapore. Because he was hardly an impartial observer, we may wish to take Lee's claims with a grain of salt. More importantly, the facts do not really fit the theory. Much of East Asia has proven very hospitable to democracy. Japan has been a democracy since the Second World War, and South Korea and Taiwan both democratized during the last two decades of the 20th century. The existence of democracy in Taiwan, where the vast majority of the population is ethnically Chinese, is a particularly strong refutation of the idea that there is something inherently undemocratic about Chinese culture.

The argument about Islam would appear, at first glance, to work better. There are no Muslim-majority democracies in the Middle East or North Africa today. Most Muslims, however, do not live in the Middle East or North Africa—and in other parts of the Islamic world, democracy has not fared as badly. Most notably, the world's biggest Muslim-majority country, Indonesia, has been more or less democratic since 1999. Even in the Middle East and North

Africa, there is apparently no lack of appetite for democracy, as evidenced by the "Arab Spring" of 2011. That year mass protests broke out in Tunisia and forced the country's long-ruling autocrat to resign. Similar protests soon swept autocrats from power in Egypt and Libya and put them on the defensive in several other countries. While only Tunisia saw democracy take root for a significant period—and even there, a self-coup in 2021 put an end to its democratic experiment—these events are hard to square with the idea of Muslims as unquestioning supporters of authoritarianism.

This chapter examines three factors that can contribute to authoritarian durability: natural resource wealth, revolutionary origins, and cross-border cooperation. These factors transcend cultural divides. Saudi Arabia is a petrostate, but so are Angola, Russia, and Venezuela. China's authoritarian regime was born of revolution, but so were those of Cuba, Iran, and Mozambique. China has served as a lifeline for North Korea, but so has Russia for Belarus and Saudi Arabia for Bahrain. However, while these factors have all bolstered authoritarian regimes, their effects may diminish over time. As the world becomes less reliant on oil, memories of revolution fade, and the foreign sponsors of authoritarianism known as "black knights" face their own challenges at home, authoritarian durability may give way to authoritarian vulnerability.

Resource curse

Discovering oil is the closest thing to winning the lottery that can happen to a country. While this might seem like the ultimate blessing, it often turns out to be a curse. Just like many lottery winners find themselves isolated and depressed, countries that discover oil or other valuable natural resources often suffer a range of harmful consequences. This is known as the "resource curse." For one, the huge influx of cash that comes from the sale of these resources can trigger the decline of other sectors of the economy, such as manufacturing and agriculture. Worse still, natural resource wealth can contribute to civil war. Because resources like oil and diamonds are so valuable, armed groups have an incentive to seek control of them. Two tragic examples are the small West African countries of Liberia and Sierra Leone, which descended into brutal civil wars during the 1990s. These wars were in large part fought over and financed by their rich diamond mines—as captured by the term "blood diamonds."

But the most relevant expression of the resource curse for our purposes is authoritarianism. This is most obvious in the case of "petrostates," or countries whose economies are heavily reliant on the export of oil. The best-known examples are countries in the Persian Gulf, such as Kuwait, the United Arab Emirates, and Saudi Arabia. However, they can also be found in Eurasia (Russia), Africa (Angola), Latin America (Venezuela), and Southeast Asia (Brunei), to name just a few examples. Many petrostates are well-off by global standards. Qatar has a higher income per capita than Germany. Nevertheless, almost none of them are democracies—a fact that would seem to fly in the face of modernization theory, which, as discussed in Chapter 5, argues that there is a relationship between development and democracy.

In his provocatively titled 2001 article "Does Oil Hinder Democracy?" the political scientist Michael L. Ross argues that there are several ways that oil can bolster authoritarian regimes. The first is the "taxation effect." When people are taxed heavily, they feel they ought to have a say in how those taxes are spent—an idea encapsulated in the slogan "no taxation without representation" during the American War of Independence. Oil revenues, however, allow petrostates to fill their coffers without having to tax their populations. Another way that oil hinders democracy is the "spending effect." Because of their wealth, petrostates can buy people's support through large-scale social spending. Oil can also hinder democracy through the "repression effect." If social spending is the carrot of petrostates, security spending is the stick. By using petrodollars to finance large, well-equipped militaries and police forces, petrostates can beat into submission anyone who cannot be bought off.

But perhaps the most interesting effect of oil is what Ross calls the "modernization effect." This is an addendum to Lipset's famous claim from Chapter 5 about more well-to-do countries being more likely to sustain democracy. That claim is only true, Ross suggests, if a country becomes well-to-do through industrialization. Modernization theory is not about how much money people have in the bank. It is about the cluster of societal changes that accompany industrialization, such as education and the growth of civil society. This is an arduous path to development and the work of generations. Petrostates take a shortcut: they drill a hole in the ground and money comes out. This can make them rich, but it does not generate the broader cluster of societal changes that sustain democracy. Oil brings wealth without modernization.

There is no better example of an authoritarian petrostate than Saudi Arabia. Since 1932, it has been an absolute monarchy and one of the world's most repressive regimes—most obviously toward women, but also toward dissidents such as the journalist Jamal Khashoggi, who was assassinated in grisly fashion by Saudi agents in 2018. What has allowed the regime to survive for so long? Much of the reason has to do with Saudi Arabia's massive oil deposits, with the taxation, spending, repression, and modernization effects all on full display. There is no personal income tax in Saudi Arabia. Social spending, however, is generous—as seen during the Arab Spring of 2011, when the government announced billions of dollars of new spending to nip potential opposition in the bud. Saudi Arabia typically spends around 10 percent of its GDP on defense—more than four times the world average. And it lacks the hallmarks of a "modern" society, with only modest education levels and a virtually non-existent civil society.

Revolutionary origins

A more recent theory of authoritarian durability highlights the role of violent revolution. The term "revolution" is used in different ways. For political scientists, though, it means something very specific: a bottom-up, violent seizure of power that leads not only to a new political regime, but also to far-reaching changes to the economy and society. Understood in this way, the 20th century saw relatively few revolutions. Examples include the Mexican Revolution of 1910–20, the Russian Revolution of 1917, the Chinese Communist Revolution of 1949, the Cuban Revolution of 1959, and the Iranian Revolution of 1979. These countries are all wildly different, as were their revolutions. They ranged from communist (Russia, China, Cuba), to Islamic (Iran), to idiosyncratic (Mexico). Despite these differences, they share a striking feature in common: they produced some of the world's most durable authoritarian regimes.

In their 2022 book *Revolution and Dictatorship: The Violent Origins of Durable Authoritarianism*, the political scientists Steven Levitsky and Lucan Way argue that this is not a coincidence. Revolutions produce a range of effects that make the regimes that emerge from them unusually resilient. The first is the destruction of rival power centers. Revolutions nearly always trigger a counter-revolutionary backlash—and, in many cases, full-blown civil war. If the counter-revolutionaries win, that is the end of the revolution. But if the revolutionaries win, they can kill or exile the organized, armed actors that pose the biggest threat to the new regime. Other potential enemies are decimated through the sorts of radical policies that revolutionary regimes tend to enact. Land reform destroys the landowning class. Churches are stripped of their assets and legal rights. The monarchy is abolished and the royal family exiled or executed. By the time the dust has settled, the country has a completely new social and economic order—one in which the revolutionary regime faces few serious threats.

The second reason why revolutionary regimes are so durable, according to Levitsky and Way, is that their ruling elites tend to be cohesive. A chronic feature of authoritarian regimes is the problem of frenemies, as discussed in Chapter 4. If factional rivalries degenerate into schisms, this can trigger the downfall of the regime. Like other authoritarian regimes, revolutionary regimes can be frightening places for those who staff them, as the victims of Stalin's purges in the Soviet Union can attest. However, they almost never experience full-blown schisms, for two reasons. First, the leaders of the revolution enjoy extraordinary legitimacy. Because figures like Lenin, Mao, and Castro are seen as national heroes, few regime officials are willing to challenge them openly. Second, the experience of revolution and civil war leads to a river of bad blood that is almost impossible to cross. It is not easy to make common cause with people who until recently were literally trying to kill you. Even discontented revolutionary regime officials are unlikely to defect to the opposition under these conditions.

Finally, revolutionary regimes tend to possess a strong and loyal coercive apparatus. Revolutions are, by definition, violent affairs. As Mao famously put it: "A revolution is not a dinner party . . . A revolution is an insurrection, an act of violence by which one class overthrows the power of another." The process of carrying out a revolution, and then defending it against its enemies, tends to result in a trustworthy military and a ruthless police force. This has two consequences. First, the new regime is "coup proof." Unlike other authoritarian regimes, revolutionary regimes almost never suffer coups. The pre-revolutionary military is dismantled, and the new one is made up of revolutionary fighters loyal to the new order. Second, the security forces are more willing to engage in what Levitsky and Way call "high-intensity coercion." To put it crudely, when push comes to shove, are they willing to machine-gun to death large numbers of peaceful protesters? While the security forces in some authoritarian regimes might balk at such an order, in those born of revolution the answer is more likely to be "yes."

10. Chinese propaganda shows a soldier holding Mao's Little Red Book.

This theory about revolutionary origins can help to explain the extraordinary durability of the People's Republic of China. The regime emerged from the 1949 Chinese Communist Revolution, the culmination of a long struggle against the ruling Chinese Nationalist Party, or KMT. The revolution had all of the effects highlighted by Levitsky and Way. In the wake of its defeat, the KMT and over a million soldiers and civilians fled mainland China for the island of Taiwan, conveniently wiping from the map the new regime's most formidable enemy. Mao emerged from decades of struggle as the regime's unrivaled leader, and after his death other revolutionary veterans like Deng Xiaoping were able to pick up the reins. Finally, decades of war resulted in a powerful and obedient military. To this day, the People's Liberation Army swears loyalty to the Chinese Communist Party, not the state. These factors enabled the regime to withstand multiple crises, including those of its own making—notably, the mass famine of the so-called Great Leap Forward (1958–62) and the chaos of the Cultural Revolution (1966–76). They also allowed it to survive the democracy protests of 1989: the bulk of the regime's leaders hung together, the army proved willing to commit mass murder, and the status quo prevailed.

Authoritarian International

A final contributor to authoritarian durability has been dubbed the "Authoritarian International." There is a long history of like-minded political parties supporting one another across borders, from the Communist International (or Comintern) created after the Russian Revolution to contemporary organizations like the Global Greens. Like-minded political regimes also have a history of providing aid and comfort to one another. After the Cold War, the United States engaged in what was called "democracy promotion," providing grants and technical assistance to election monitors, independent media, and civil society organizations in fledgling democracies. The European Union provided similar support, especially to the new democracies of Eastern Europe. But it was not just democracies that worked together. Authoritarian regimes also did their best to make the world safe for autocracy. While they did not form a literal organization equivalent to the Comintern, they cooperated with one another in a variety of ways.

One kind of authoritarian cooperation takes the form of "black knights." Black knights are bigger, more powerful authoritarian regimes that prop up smaller, less powerful ones. A good example is China's support for North Korea. The relationship between the neighboring communist regimes goes back to the time of the Korean War (1950–3), when millions of Chinese soldiers fought on the side of North Korea. They became so close that, according to one saying, they were like "lips and teeth." The two countries signed a mutual defense treaty, and China eventually became North Korea's biggest trade partner. After it developed nuclear weapons in 2006, North Korea became an international pariah and the target of severe economic sanctions. However, while

China sometimes expressed frustration with its junior partner, it continued to trade with North Korea and acted as a crucial lifeline by providing it with food and other assistance.

Russia under Vladimir Putin has played a similar black knight role. Putin famously described the collapse of the Soviet Union as "the greatest geopolitical catastrophe" of the 20th century, and set about trying to restore Russian influence in other post-Soviet states. One country where Russia's support was critical is Belarus, which during the decades-long rule of Alexander Lukashenko became known as "Europe's last dictatorship." In 2020, after presidential elections gave Lukashenko an implausibly large margin of victory, nationwide protests threatened the regime's survival. However, Lukashenko muddled through—thanks, in large part, to financial support from Russia and offers of military assistance. In an op-ed published later, the main Belarusian opposition leader and likely winner of the disputed election stated the view of many when she wrote: "Lukashenko would not have survived the uprising that followed the stolen 2020 election if it wasn't for Vladimir Putin."

In addition to bigger authoritarian regimes propping up smaller ones in their spheres of influence, authoritarian regimes can engage in peer-to-peer cooperation. One example from the Cold War is Operation Condor, when right-wing military regimes in South America joined forces to hunt down each other's enemies. A more recent example is the partnership struck up between China and Russia in February 2022, which their leaders described as having "no limits." The real-world implications of this partnership became clear just a few weeks later when Russia launched a full-scale invasion of Ukraine. In response, the United States, the European Union, and other democracies such as Japan imposed massive sanctions on Russia and tried to wean themselves off Russian energy exports. China came to the rescue, dramatically increasing its purchase of Russia's oil and helping it to obtain much-needed goods. In exchange, Russia lent its support to China as it ramped up its saber-rattling toward Taiwan, which China regards as a rogue province and has pledged to bring under Beijing's control.

A final form of international cooperation is less direct: authoritarian regimes can learn from each other. The Chinese Communist Party, for example, has closely studied the collapse of the Soviet Union and sought to avoid what it views as Gorbachev's mistakes—most importantly, his decision to pair economic reform with greater political freedom, as discussed in Chapter 5. It has also sent thousands of officials to study the "Singapore model," in an effort to understand how Singapore managed to become the only country in the world that is both fully developed and authoritarian (with the exception of petrostates). For his part, Putin learned from a wave of mass uprisings in post-communist countries known as the "Color Revolutions." These saw the toppling of autocrats in Georgia (2003), Ukraine (2004), and Kyrgyzstan (2005), leading to hopes—or fears—that Russia would be next. The lesson that Putin seems to have learned from these uprisings is that "if you give an inch, they'll take a mile." He responded by clamping down on Russian NGOs, independent media, and opposition parties. If until the mid-2000s Russia was an example of what Levitsky and Way call competitive authoritarianism, thereafter the competitive part all but disappeared.

From durability to vulnerability?

The puzzle of authoritarian durability becomes less puzzling when we take into account factors such as oil, revolution, and authoritarian cooperation. This does not mean that autocrats can breathe easy, however. Durability is not immortality. At least two of the sources of authoritarian durability discussed in this chapter would seem to have built-in expiration dates. To the extent that petrostates rely on the logic of "no oil, no autocracy," their leaders should be worried. There is pressure on all countries to move to clean energy in order to limit the worst effects of climate change. If in a hypothetical green future there ceases to be the same voracious appetite for oil as there is today, authoritarian regimes such as Russia and Saudi Arabia could be in trouble. Even if the world never quits oil, oil will eventually quit the countries that produce it. No oil well is bottomless.

Revolutionary regimes face their own long-term difficulties. As their founding leaders die off and memories of the revolution fade, they begin to lose their special sources of durability. Some have made the transition from revolutionary to post-revolutionary regime more successfully than others. In the Soviet Union, Gorbachev hoped that glasnost and perestroika would lead to increased prosperity and thus greater support for communism. They had the opposite effect, triggering the regime's downfall. The free-market reforms carried out by China after 1978 were far more effective. They set in motion what the World Bank described as the "fastest sustained expansion by a major economy in history," lifting hundreds of millions of people out of poverty and generating significant good will for the Chinese Communist Party. However, as discussed in Chapter 4, staking an authoritarian regime's legitimacy on economic performance is a risky bet. The good times cannot last forever.

The long-term implications of authoritarian cooperation are more mixed. Authoritarian learning and peer-to-peer cooperation are unlikely ever to go away. The impact of black knights like China and Russia, however, may diminish over time. Currently, these countries not only wield power directly in countries like North Korea and Belarus, but also have broader influence through regional organizations such as the Commonwealth of Independent States, an association of post-Soviet countries (not to be confused with the Commonwealth of Nations, a club for former British colonies), and the Shanghai Cooperation Organization, a China-led body of mostly authoritarian regimes. Saudi Arabia plays a similar black knight role in countries like Bahrain, as well as leading its own international club for autocracies, the Gulf Cooperation Council. Russia, China, and Saudi Arabia are the pillars of authoritarianism in their respective regions. If those pillars were ever to fall due to factors such as declining oil revenues or an economic slowdown, it could threaten the entire edifice.

Chapter 7
Legacies of authoritarianism

The American novelist William Faulkner once wrote: "The past is never dead. It's not even past." The same is true of authoritarian regimes. Even in countries that democratize, legacies of authoritarianism almost always live on in one form or another. The type of legacy that readers are most likely to be familiar with is the unhealed wound of human rights abuses. One horrific example is the so-called "Dirty War" unleashed by Argentina's last military regime (1976–83), in which between 9,000 and 30,000 people were killed—some of them dropped from airplanes, drugged, into the ocean. The fact that estimates of the number killed vary so wildly hints at one of the cruelest parts of this legacy: the uncertainty. Many victims' families never get a clear answer about what happened to their loved ones. There is no grave, no paper trail, no closure. They simply disappear.

Making matters worse is the lack of accountability. Here Argentina is actually an outlier: after the return of democracy in 1983, it held what became known as the "Trial of the Juntas," in which several top leaders of the military regime were given long prison sentences. More common was what happened in Spain after Franco's death in 1975, where a consensus emerged not to dredge up the past. This was informally known as the "Pact of Forgetting." The case of Indonesia is even more disturbing. In 1965–6, the country's military launched a wave of mass murder against Communist Party members and alleged sympathizers, killing between 500,000 and one million people. In the late 1990s, after three decades of authoritarian rule, Indonesia democratized, but there would be no justice for the victims. As explored in the 2012 documentary *The Act of Killing*, some of the killers became public figures, boasting in chilling detail about the precise ways they used pieces of wire to strangle their victims to death.

This chapter focuses on two less familiar but equally common authoritarian legacies: constitutions and political parties. In many countries, authoritarian officials play a key role in writing the constitutions of new democratic regimes—constitutions that often lock in privileges for elites at the expense of voters. However, this is not just a story about voters being trampled upon. Those very voters often choose, voluntarily, to vote the "bad guys" back into office. Given the option of voting for anyone they please, they cast their ballots for former authoritarian ruling parties or new parties created by former authoritarian officials. These legacies not only raise uncomfortable questions about issues like popular support for authoritarian regimes, but also present dilemmas for democratic governments.

Holdover constitutions

One common authoritarian legacy comes in the form of constitutions. A constitution is a country's basic law. It lays out how governments are formed, how laws are made, and what rights citizens enjoy. It is also meant to be permanent. This makes the stakes high when writing a new constitution—which is why it is so startling that many of the world's democratic constitutions were written, in whole or in part, by authoritarian officials. Sometimes this is the result of the pact-making process, with outgoing officials negotiating provisions designed to protect their vital interests, as discussed in Chapter 5. Other times they do not even need to negotiate: they are strong enough simply to impose a constitution to their liking, regardless of what the opposition may think of it. Either way, the result is that many new democracies begin their lives with what the political scientist Terry Lynn Karl calls a "birth defect."

How common are these constitutional birth defects? In their 2018 book *Authoritarianism and the Elite Origins of Democracy*, the political scientists Michael Albertus and Victor Menaldo take up this question by examining every case of democratization in the world from 1800 to 2006. They find that in two-thirds of cases, the new democracy inherited its constitution from the former authoritarian regime. They call these "holdover constitutions." Examples include South Korea, whose constitution in its current form was introduced by the military authorities in 1987; Ghana, whose constitution was imposed by autocrat Jerry Rawlings in 1992; and Peru, whose constitution was approved in 1993 in the wake of a self-coup by Alberto Fujimori. All of these countries became democracies—but with rules imposed by autocrats.

Holdover constitutions are often designed to weaken the power of voters. Electoral rules are tailor-made to favor the rich or other groups associated with the old regime. Laws on hot-button issues like taxation and property rights require legislative super-majorities. The tools of direct democracy, such as citizen initiatives, are banned. In extreme cases, competition itself and the ability of elected governments to govern are constrained: certain kinds of political parties are banned, unelected bodies are granted veto powers, and the armed forces are not subject to civilian control. The sociologist and political scientist Manuel Antonio Garretón called such restrictions "authoritarian enclaves." If enough of them are baked into a constitution, it is reasonable to ask whether the regime deserves to be called a democracy at all.

One example of a holdover constitution rife with authoritarian enclaves is Chile. In 1988, as discussed in Chapter 5, a plebiscite was held to determine whether Pinochet, in power since the 1973 coup, should remain in office. A majority of Chileans voted "no," new elections were held, and military rule came to an end. The constitution of Chile's new democracy, however, was not written by democrats. It was imposed in 1980 by the military regime and laid out a vision for what its authors called "protected democracy." The people, they believed, needed to be protected from themselves, which the constitution sought to do through various means: the Senate would be partially appointed, Marxist parties would be banned, and an unelected committee dominated by the military would have far-reaching powers. The armed forces would also enjoy broad autonomy over their own affairs. To add insult to injury, Pinochet stayed on as head of the army until 1998, a full eight years after the end of military rule.

The good news is that many holdover constitutions are eventually replaced or amended in a more democratic direction. In the case of Chile, this began immediately after the 1988 plebiscite, with negotiations between the democratic opposition and moderate supporters of the military regime softening some of the constitution's most outrageous features. Over the years, additional constitutional amendments steadily eroded the remaining authoritarian enclaves. In 2022, Chileans were finally given the opportunity to vote in a plebiscite on whether to replace the constitution with a progressive new one written by a popularly elected assembly. Over 60 percent of Chileans voted against the new constitution, apparently preferring the devil they knew. In 2023, they rejected another draft constitution, this time a conservative one. While the choice to retain Pinochet's constitution surprised many observers, it was ultimately a democratic decision. For better or worse, this is what a majority of Chileans wanted.

Authoritarian successor parties

A second common legacy comes in the form of "authoritarian successor parties." These are parties that emerge from authoritarian regimes, but that continue to operate after a transition to democracy. Sometimes they are former authoritarian ruling parties that simply continue to exist. One example is Poland. During the 1980s, a mass social movement, Solidarity, emerged in opposition to the country's communist regime, as discussed in Chapter 5. In 1989, the communist authorities allowed competitive legislative elections for the first time—and lost by a landslide. The victory of Solidarity in these elections set in motion a transition to democracy, the inspiring climax of a decade-long story. Less inspiring was the story's epilogue: in 1993, in an apparent fit of buyer's remorse, Polish voters decided to return the old communist party to power. Some version of this story played out in most post-communist democracies. The same occurred in non-communist cases, too, such as Ghana, Mexico, and Taiwan, with voters using their newfound democratic rights to return former authoritarian ruling parties to power.

In other countries, authoritarian successor parties are what we might call "inside-out" parties: they are new parties formed by regime insiders on the way out in order to retain influence in the new regime. One example is Spain. During the transition to democracy in the 1970s, former Franco officials launched not one but two new parties. The first was led by softliners and briefly dominated national politics, before collapsing in the 1980s. The second was led by hardliners and eventually took the name People's Party, or PP. The PP became one of Spain's two main parties, winning office on multiple occasions. Two authoritarian successor parties corresponding to the softliner/hardliner divide also emerged in Chile. The first, National Renewal, has won the presidency twice. Its coalition partner, the Independent Democratic Union, or UDI, has been a vociferous defender of the Pinochet legacy, usually coming in first or second place in legislative elections.

While the existence of authoritarian successor parties may be counter-intuitive, they are one of the most common features of the global democratic landscape. In research for my 2018 co-edited book *Life after Dictatorship: Authoritarian Successor Parties Worldwide*, I looked at every country in the world that democratized between 1974 and 2010 to see whether an authoritarian successor party emerged and, if so, whether it returned to power. The results were stunning: in nearly *three-quarters* of cases, a prominent authoritarian successor party emerged. And in over *one-half* of countries that democratized during this period, an authoritarian successor party was voted back into office. These parties were especially common in post-communist Europe, returning to power in a whopping two-thirds of cases. They were also widespread in Africa, Asia, and Latin America, as well as in Tunisia during its decade of democracy following the Arab Spring of 2011.

The success of these parties cannot be explained by electoral manipulation, since, to be considered an authoritarian successor party, the party must operate in a real democracy. (Authoritarian regimes that hold multi-party elections, such as Russia, Singapore, or Zimbabwe, are therefore excluded.) Nor is this a story of collective amnesia on the part of voters. These parties often go out of their way to remind people where they come from and what they stand for. On International Human Rights Day in 2014, for example, legislators from Chile's UDI called for a moment of silence—not for the victims of the military regime, but in honor of Pinochet. Another example is Panama's Democratic Revolutionary Party, or PRD. Founded under left-wing military rule in the 1970s, the PRD became the country's most important political party after the United States invaded in 1989–90 and imposed democracy. In 1999 and 2004, the party ran Martín Torrijos, the son of former autocrat Omar Torrijos, as its candidate (he won the second time). To this day, the PRD's symbol is an "O" with an "11" inside, a reference to the coup of October 11, 1968, that brought the military to power.

Benefits of an authoritarian past

How is it possible for a party with roots in authoritarianism to thrive under democracy? Why are authoritarian successor parties so common? According to the political scientist Anna Grzymala-Busse, these parties often benefit from a "usable past." Whether we like it or not, many authoritarian regimes have a bedrock of popular support. Sometimes this is rooted in "negative legitimacy," with people rallying behind autocrats in the face of a perceived threat, as discussed in Chapter 4. If that threat persists after a transition to democracy, this can translate into electoral support for authoritarian successor parties. In Chile, for example, the return of democracy also saw the return of the main leftist parties of the Allende government, including Allende's Socialist Party. Fearing a return to what they viewed as the "bad old days," many voters threw their support to the UDI, the party most closely tied to the Pinochet regime.

In other cases, popular support for authoritarian regimes is rooted in their performance. While most authoritarian regimes do not govern particularly well, some can point to real accomplishments. As the parties most closely associated with the old regime, this can give authoritarian successor parties a strong brand to run on under democracy. Two clear examples are the KMT regime in Taiwan and the military regime of Park Chung-hee in South Korea, which, as noted in Chapter 4, both oversaw economic miracles. In 2000, the KMT lost the presidency and Taiwan democratized. Eight years later, Taiwanese voters returned the KMT to power. It remains one of the island's two main parties to this day. In South Korea, the party formed by Park Chung-hee under military rule likewise thrived after the transition to democracy in the late 1980s. In 2012, its successful presidential candidate was none other than Park Geun-hye, the late autocrat's daughter. In an unsubtle reference to the most famous slogan from her father's regime, "Try to Live Well," one of her campaign slogans was "Try to Live Well, Again."

A final factor is nostalgia, whether rooted in reality or fantasy. The passage of time has a way of whitewashing the past. The good comes to the fore, and the bad fades from memory. Even in

11. Park Geun-hye visits her dictator father's grave the day after winning South Korea's 2012 presidential election.

countries where the old regime could not claim accomplishments comparable to those of Taiwan and South Korea, this can benefit authoritarian successor parties—especially when people's high hopes for democracy have not been realized. One example is Mexico. In 2000, after seven decades of hegemonic-party rule, the PRI lost the presidency and the country democratized. The results, however, were disappointing: economic performance was mediocre, and a bloody drug war killed thousands. This created an opening for the PRI, whose successful 2012 presidential candidate ran with the slogan "You know me," a winking nod to the bygone days of PRI rule. Similar considerations helped Ferdinand "Bongbong" Marcos, Jr., the son of former autocrat Ferdinand Marcos, to win the 2022 presidential election in the Philippines. On the campaign trail, he praised his famously corrupt father as a "genius," and pledged to restore the supposed golden age of peace and prosperity of the Marcos years.

As the examples of Bongbong Marcos, Park Geun-hye, and Martín Torrijos illustrate, nostalgia and/or a real record of accomplishment can provide an opening for the family members of former autocrats. They can even provide an opening for former autocrats themselves. One example is Bolivia, which democratized in the early 1980s after years of military rule. The transition to democracy, however, coincided with a hyperinflationary economic crisis. This allowed Hugo Banzer, a former military ruler (1971–8), to attempt a comeback. His pitch to voters was not subtle: he ran newspaper advertisements comparing everything from unemployment to the price of bread during and after his regime, promising to recreate his past achievements if elected. Banzer became a central player in Bolivia's democracy, eventually returning to the presidency in 1997—this time at the invitation of voters. Multiple countries have sent former autocrats back to power in democratic elections, including Benin, the Dominican Republic, Madagascar, Nicaragua, and Nigeria (twice). Because their ties to the old regime are so unmistakable, these figures help to clarify why actors with authoritarian pasts so often win democratic elections: they win because of those pasts, not despite them.

Dilemmas of authoritarian legacies

These legacies of authoritarianism present dilemmas for which there are no simple solutions. The least complicated, at least in principle, is the issue of human rights: murder and torture are wrong, full stop. Those responsible should face justice. Yet while the moral calculus is clear, the practical one can be murky. Democratization is not a one-way street. There is always the risk of a return to authoritarianism, especially if actors from the old regime feel they are being treated unfairly. This risk was on full display after the transition to democracy in Chile, with Pinochet declaring: "The day they touch one of my men, the rule of law ends." In 1993, Pinochet even sent troops into the streets of the capital to warn against possible investigations of his family for corruption. In Argentina, the pushback was even more dramatic: there were four bloody military revolts between 1987 and 1990. Eventually, the Argentine government backed down and granted pardons to those responsible for human rights abuses during the Dirty War.

Holdover constitutions also pose a dilemma. The illegitimacy of their origins and the questionable provisions they often contain make the moral case for abolishing them straightforward. Once again, however, there may be pragmatic reasons to hold back. These constitutions are designed to protect the vital interests of powerful actors—actors who, if they believe those interests to be in danger, may turn against democracy. There is an additional reason for caution: constitutional engineering is often used by populists to entrench themselves in power. As noted in Chapter 2, these are politicians who present themselves as champions of the common people against the corrupt elite. One populist tactic is to call for a constituent assembly to write a new constitution—and then to use it to bypass the legislature, purge the judiciary, and stack the electoral authorities. This was the playbook followed, for example, by Hugo Chávez in Venezuela after winning the 1998 presidential election. He immediately convened a constituent assembly that, in the words of one observer, "declared itself legally omnipotent." This allowed Chávez to sidestep checks and balances and put the country on the road to authoritarianism.

The final dilemma is the one posed by authoritarian successor parties. There is something inherently offensive about former authoritarian officials running for office, loudly and proudly, under democracy. Banning them, however, is no solution. These parties often have significant popular support, including from powerful actors who could become democratic "spoilers" if they decided to. The least bad option for democrats may be simply to hold their noses and tolerate these parties, provided they do not engage in blatantly disloyal behavior. The good news is that most do not. Authoritarian successor parties are ubiquitous, yet in only a handful of cases has their election triggered a democratic breakdown. Over time, they typically come to resemble "normal" parties—to such an extent, in fact, that we sometimes lose sight of their undemocratic origins altogether. The Conservative Party in Great Britain, for example, emerged during the country's pre-democratic past to represent elite interests. It is an example of what the political scientist Daniel Ziblatt calls an "old regime conservative party," a historical cousin of today's authoritarian successor parties. These parties are an unseemly, but ultimately normal, part of democracy. The best approach to them is live and let live.

For the other two legacies of authoritarianism—the unhealed wound of human rights abuses and holdover constitutions—the least bad option may be slow and steady. The great German sociologist Max Weber famously wrote: "Politics is a strong and slow boring of hard boards. It takes both passion and perspective." Both are needed when dealing with authoritarian legacies. Democratic activists must keep their eyes on the prize of improving democracy, while also recognizing that this is the work of years if not decades. Chile's first democratically elected president after military rule, Patricio Aylwin, captured this idea when he promised to pursue justice for the victims of military rule "to the extent possible." This was not cynicism, but pragmatism. Over the years, what was deemed possible began to change—particularly after Pinochet was arrested by British police in 1998 while in London for a medical procedure. When Pinochet later returned to Chile, he was no longer the untouchable figure that he had been previously. The country's judges became bolder in their pursuit of human rights abusers, and politicians enacted increasingly far-reaching constitutional reforms. Slowly but surely, justice advanced, and bit by bit, the hard boards of authoritarianism were whittled away.

References

Preface

Karl Marx and Friedrich Engels, *The Communist Manifesto* (Oxford: Oxford University Press, 1992 [1848]), 2

Chapter 1: What is authoritarianism?

Theodor W. Adorno, Else Frenkel-Brunswik, Daniel J. Levinson, and R. Nevitt Sanford, *The Authoritarian Personality* (London: Verso, 2019 [1950])

Hannah Arendt, *The Origins of Totalitarianism* (Great Britain: Penguin Books, 2017 [1951])

"eclectic hodge-podge": Stanley G. Payne, *Franco's Spain* (London: Routledge & Kegan Paul, 1968), 24

Juan J. Linz, "An Authoritarian Regime: Spain," in Erik Allardt and Yrjö Littunen, eds., *Cleavages, Ideologies, and Party Systems: Contributions to Comparative Political Sociology* (Helsinki: The Academic Bookstore, 1964)

Juan J. Linz, *Totalitarian and Authoritarian Regimes* (Boulder, CO: Lynne Rienner Publishers, 2000 [1975])

Milan W. Svolik, *The Politics of Authoritarian Rule* (New York: Cambridge University Press, 2012), 22

Samuel P. Huntington, *The Third Wave: Democratization in the Late Twentieth Century* (Norman: University of Oklahoma Press, 1991)

Francis Fukuyama, *The End of History and the Last Man* (New York: Avon Books, 1992) "electoralist fallacy": Juan J. Linz and Alfred Stepan, *Problems of Democratic Transition and Consolidation: Southern Europe, South America, and Post-Communist Europe* (Baltimore: The Johns Hopkins University Press, 1996), 4

Robert A. Dahl, *Polyarchy: Participation and Opposition* (New Haven: Yale University Press, 1971)

"crimes against humanity": quoted in Nick Cumming-Bruce and Austin Ramzy, "U.N. says China may have committed 'crimes against humanity' in Xinjiang," *The New York Times*, August 31, 2022

"admitted that it had been rigged": Ginger Thompson, "Ex-President in Mexico casts new light on rigged 1988 election," *The New York Times*, March 9, 2004

"illegal public protest": "Public order in Singapore has been shaken by a hand-drawn smiley face," *The Economist*, November 26, 2020

Chapter 2: Varieties of authoritarianism

"20,000 Republican prisoners": Paul Preston, *The Spanish Holocaust: Inquisition and Extermination in Twentieth-Century Spain* (London: Harper Press, 2012), xi

"low hundreds": based on data from the Museu do Aljube—Resistência e Liberdade (Lisbon, Portugal)

Adam Przeworski, *Democracy and the Market: Political and Economic Reforms in Eastern Europe and Latin America* (Cambridge: Cambridge University Press, 1991), 10

"premier pharmacist": quoted in Lisa Wedeen, *Ambiguities of Domination: Politics, Rhetoric, and Symbols in Contemporary Syria* (Chicago: University of Chicago Press, 1999), 1. Other authoritarian self-descriptions in this chapter come from press accounts.

"conjugal dictatorship": Primitivo Mijares, cited in Mark R. Thompson, *The Anti-Marcos Struggle: Personalistic Rule and Democratic Transition in the Philippines* (New Haven: Yale University Press, 1995), 69

Steven Levitsky and Lucan A. Way, *Competitive Authoritarianism: Hybrid Regimes After the Cold War* (New York: Cambridge University Press, 2010), 12

"around 15 percent": Steven Levitsky and Lucan Way, "The New Competitive Authoritarianism," *Journal of Democracy*, 31, 1 (2020) "electoral autocracy": V-Dem, quoted in Soutik Biswas, "'Electoral autocracy': The downgrading of India's democracy," *BBC News*, March 16, 2021

Chapter 3: The birth of authoritarian regimes

"10–20 percent": Kurt A. Raaflaub, "Introduction," in Kurt A. Raaflaub, Josiah Ober, and Robert W. Wallace, *Origins of Democracy in Ancient Greece* (Berkeley: University of California Press, 2007), 11

Juan J. Linz, *The Breakdown of Democratic Regimes: Crisis, Breakdown, and Reequilibration* (Baltimore: The Johns Hopkins University Press, 1978)

Steven Levitsky and Daniel Ziblatt, *How Democracies Die* (New York: Crown, 2018)

"all but inviting": Arturo Valenzuela, *The Breakdown of Democratic Regimes: Chile* (Baltimore: The Johns Hopkins University Press, 1978), 104

Kurt Weyland, *Assault on Democracy: Communism, Fascism, and Authoritarianism During the Interwar Years* (New York: Cambridge University Press, 2021)

"armed struggle": quoted in Kenneth M. Roberts, *Deepening Democracy? The Modern Left and Social Movements in Chile and Peru* (Stanford, CA: Stanford University Press, 1998), 92

Pamela Constable and Arturo Valenzuela, *A Nation of Enemies: Chile Under Pinochet* (New York: W. W. Norton & Company, 1991)

Amartya Sen, "Democracy as a Universal Value," *Journal of Democracy*, 10, 3 (1999)

Chapter 4: The life of authoritarian regimes

Jeff Goodwin, *No Other Way Out: States and Revolutionary Movements, 1945–1991* (New York: Cambridge University Press, 2001)

Huntington, *The Third Wave*, 46–58

Timur Kuran, "Now Out of Never: The Element of Surprise in the East European Revolution of 1989," *World Politics*, 44, 1 (1991)

"dictator trap": Brian Klaas, "Vladimir Putin has fallen into the dictator trap," *The Atlantic*, March 16, 2022

"fantasy world": Mykhailo Podolyak, quoted in Luke Harding, "A day after it was 'annexed', crucial city returned to Ukraine," *The Observer*, October 2, 2022

Martin K. Dimitrov, *Dictatorship and Information: Authoritarian Resilience in Communist Europe and China* (New York: Oxford University Press, 2022)

Martin K. Dimitrov, "What the Party Wanted to Know: Citizen Complaints as a 'Barometer of Public Opinion' in Communist Bulgaria," *East European Politics and Societies*, 28, 2 (2014)

Guillermo O'Donnell and Philippe C. Schmitter, *Transitions from Authoritarian Rule: Tentative Conclusions about Uncertain Democracies* (Baltimore: The Johns Hopkins University Press, 1986), 19

Barbara Geddes, "What Do We Know About Democratization After Twenty Years?" *Annual Review of Political Science*, 2 (1999)

Andrea Kendall-Taylor and Erica Frantz, "When Dictators Die," *Journal of Democracy*, 27, 4 (2016)

Jason Brownlee, "Hereditary Succession in Modern Autocracies," *World Politics*, 59, 4 (2007)

Chapter 5: The death of authoritarian regimes

Seymour Martin Lipset, "Some Social Requisites of Democracy: Economic Development and Political Legitimacy," *American Political Science Review*, 53, 1 (1959), 75

John Donne, "No Man Is an Island" (1624); updated to modern spelling

Huntington, *The Third Wave*, 72–100

"error has no rights": quoted in John Cogley, "Freedom of religion; Vatican decree supplants ancient doctrine that 'error has no rights,'" *The New York Times*, December 8, 1965

"Catholic wave": Daniel Philpott, "Christianity and Democracy: The Catholic Wave," *Journal of Democracy*, 15, 2 (2004)

"free Poland": Alexander Kwásniewski, quoted in Richard Bernstein, "Pope helped bring Poland its freedom," *The New York Times*, April 6, 2005

"tried to cling to power": "Chile's Gen Pinochet 'tried to cling to power' in 1988," *BBC News*, February 24, 2013

"In Poland, it took ten years": slightly paraphrased from Huntington, *The Third Wave*, 105

"including Nelson Mandela": Stephen Ellis, "Nelson Mandela, the South African Communist Party and the Origins of Umkhonto we Sizwe," *Cold War History*, 16, 1 (2016) "window of opportunity": "Interview with President F. W. de Klerk," in Sergio Bitar and Abraham F. Lowenthal, eds., *Democratic Transitions: Conversations with World Leaders* (Baltimore: The Johns Hopkins University Press, 2015), 315

Dahl, *Polyarchy*, 15–16

"terrorism watch list": Robert Windrem, "US government considered Nelson Mandela a terrorist until 2008," *NBC News*, December 7, 2013

O'Donnell and Schmitter, *Transitions from Authoritarian Rule*, 37–8

"Faustian": Ronnie Kasrils, "How the ANC's Faustian pact sold out South Africa's poorest," *The Guardian*, June 24, 2013

Linz and Stepan, *Problems of Democratic Transition and Consolidation*, 5

"one man, one vote, one time": Fareed Zakaria, *The Future of Freedom: Illiberal Democracy at Home and Abroad* (New York: W. W. Norton & Company, 2003), 121

"greatest man in the world": quoted in Seymour Martin Lipset, "George Washington and the Founding of Democracy," *Journal of Democracy*, 9, 4 (1998), 24

Chapter 6: The puzzle of authoritarian durability

Michael L. Ross, "Does Oil Hinder Democracy?" *World Politics*, 53, 3 (2001)

"announced billions of dollars": Neil MacFarquhar, "In Saudi Arabia, royal funds buy peace for now," *The New York Times*, June 8, 2011

Steven Levitsky and Lucan Way, *Revolution and Dictatorship: The Violent Origins of Durable Authoritarianism* (Princeton: Princeton University Press, 2022)

"dinner party": quoted in Delia Davin, *Mao: A Very Short Introduction* (Oxford: Oxford University Press, 2013), 21

"Authoritarian International": Vitali Silitski, quoted in Lucan Ahmad Way, "The Rebirth of the Liberal World Order?," *Journal of Democracy*, 33, 2 (2022), 12

"black knights": term first coined by Gary Clyde Hufbauer, Jeffrey J. Schott, and Kimberly Ann Elliott, as discussed in Jakob Tolstrup, "Black Knights and Elections in Authoritarian Regimes: Why and How Russia Supports Authoritarian Incumbents in Post-Soviet States," *European Journal of Political Research*, 54, 4 (2015)

"greatest geopolitical catastrophe": quoted in "Putin deplores collapse of USSR," *BBC News*, April 25, 2005

"Lukashenko would not have survived": Sviatlana Tsikhanouskaya, "Putin's ally stole my democratic victory in Belarus. Now the west must help us fight back," *The Guardian*, September 17, 2022

"Singapore model": Stephan Ortmann and Mark R. Thompson, "China and the 'Singapore Model,'" *Journal of Democracy*, 27, 1 (2016)

"fastest sustained expansion": quoted in Yuen Yuen Ang, *China's Gilded Age: The Paradox of Economic Boom and Vast Corruption* (New York: Cambridge University Press, 2020), 2

Chapter 7: Legacies of authoritarianism

William Faulkner, *Requiem for a Nun* (New York: Random House, 1951), 92

Terry Lynn Karl, "Dilemmas of Democratization in Latin America," *Comparative Politics*, 23, 1 (1990), 8

Michael Albertus and Victor Menaldo, *Authoritarianism and the Elite Origins of Democracy* (New York: Cambridge University Press, 2018)

Manuel Antonio Garretón, *Incomplete Democracy: Political Democratization in Chile and Latin America* (Chapel Hill: University of North Carolina Press, 2003)

James Loxton, "Introduction: Authoritarian Successor Parties Worldwide," in James Loxton and Scott Mainwaring, eds., *Life After Dictatorship: Authoritarian Successor Parties Worldwide* (New York: Cambridge University Press, 2018)

Anna M. Grzymala-Busse, *Redeeming the Communist Past: The Regeneration of Communist Parties in East Central Europe* (Cambridge: Cambridge University Press, 2002)

"Try to Live Well, Again": quoted in Hyejin Kim, "A Link to the Authoritarian Past? Older Voters as a Force in the 2012 South Korean Presidential Election," *Taiwan Journal of Democracy*, 10, 2 (2014), 59. Other descriptions of politicians' words and behavior in this chapter come from press accounts.

"The day they touch one of my men": quoted in Jonathan Kandell, "Augusto Pinochet, dictator who ruled by terror in Chile, dies at 91," *The New York Times*, December 11, 2006

"legally omnipotent": Michael Coppedge, "Venezuela: Popular Sovereignty versus Liberal Democracy," in Jorge I. Domínguez and Michael Shifter, eds., *Constructing Democratic Governance in*

Latin America, 2nd edition (Baltimore: The Johns Hopkins University Press, 2003), 187

Daniel Ziblatt, "Reluctant Democrats: Old Regime Conservative Parties in Democracy's First Wave in Europe," in Loxton and Mainwaring, eds., *Life After Dictatorship*

Max Weber, "Politics as a Vocation," in H. H. Gerth and C. Wright Mills, eds., *From Max Weber: Essays in Sociology* (London: Routledge & Kegan Paul, 1948 [1919]), 128

Further reading

Preface

On the growing threat of authoritarianism in the 21st century, see
Larry Diamond, *Ill Winds: Saving Democracy from Russian Rage,
Chinese Ambition, and American Complacency* (New York:
Penguin Press, 2019).

Chapter 1: What is authoritarianism?

For biographical details on Linz, see Juan J. Linz, "Between Nations
and Disciplines: Personal Experience and Intellectual
Understanding of Societies and Political Regimes," in Hans
Daalder, ed., *Comparative European Politics: The Story of a
Profession* (London: Pinter, 1997); and "Juan J. Linz: Political
Regimes and the Quest for Knowledge," in Gerardo L. Munck and
Richard Snyder, *Passion, Craft, and Method in Comparative
Politics* (Baltimore: The Johns Hopkins University Press, 2007).

On the procedural minimum definition of democracy and the
electoralist fallacy, see Philippe C. Schmitter and Terry Lynn Karl,
"What Democracy Is . . . and Is Not," *Journal of Democracy*, 2, 3
(1991). For alternative ways to conceptualize democracy, and for
global trends over time, see Michael Coppedge et al., *Varieties of
Democracy: Measuring Two Centuries of Political Change*
(Cambridge: Cambridge University Press, 2020).

For more on some of the regimes discussed in this chapter, see Jane
Caplan, *Nazi Germany: A Very Short Introduction* (Oxford: Oxford
University Press, 2019); Stephen Lovell, *The Soviet Union: A Very*

Short Introduction (Oxford: Oxford University Press, 2009);
Stanley G. Payne, *The Franco Regime, 1936–1975* (London:
Phoenix Press, 2000); Martin K. Bradley, *Under the Loving Care of
the Fatherly Leader: North Korea and the Kim Dynasty* (New York:
Thomas Dunne Books, 2004); Susan L. Shirk, *Overreach: How
China Derailed Its Peaceful Rise* (New York: Oxford University Press,
2023); and Timothy Frye, *Weak Strongman: The Limits of Power in
Putin's Russia* (Princeton: Princeton University Press, 2021).

Chapter 2: Varieties of authoritarianism

For data on different kinds of authoritarian regime and regime
transitions between 1946 and 2010, see Barbara Geddes, Joseph
Wright, and Erica Frantz, "Autocratic Breakdown and Regime
Transitions: A New Data Set," *Perspectives on Politics*, 12, 2 (2014).
This data set is publicly available and can be accessed here:
<https://sites.psu.edu/dictators/>.

On Leninist parties, see chapters 1 and 3 of Leslie Holmes,
Communism: A Very Short Introduction (New York: Oxford
University Press, 2009).

For more on some of the regimes discussed in this chapter, see
Gerardo L. Munck, *Authoritarianism and Democratization:
Soldiers and Workers in Argentina, 1976–1983* (University Park,
PA: Pennsylvania State University Press, 1998); Beatriz Magaloni,
*Voting for Autocracy: Hegemonic Party Survival and Its Demise in
Mexico* (New York: Cambridge University Press, 2006); Michela
Wrong, *In the Footsteps of Mr. Kurtz: Living on the Brink of
Disaster in Mobutu's Congo* (New York: Perennial, 2002); and
Catherine M. Conaghan, *Fujimori's Peru: Deception in the Public
Sphere* (Pittsburgh: University of Pittsburgh Press, 2005). On
Marcos in the Philippines, Trujillo in the Dominican Republic,
the Somozas in Nicaragua, and the Duvaliers in Haiti, see chapters
in H. E. Chehabi and Juan J. Linz, eds., *Sultanistic Regimes*
(Baltimore: The Johns Hopkins University Press, 1998).

On democratic backsliding in India, see Christophe Jaffrelot, *Modi's
India: Hindu Nationalism and the Rise of Ethnic Democracy*
(Princeton: Princeton University Press, 2021). On the United
States, see Steven Levitsky and Daniel Ziblatt, *The Tyranny of the
Minority: Why American Democracy Reached the Breaking Point*
(New York: Crown, 2023).

On populism, see Cas Mudde and Cristóbal Rovira Kaltwasser, *Populism: A Very Short Introduction* (New York: Oxford University Press, 2017). On how populism can contribute to democratic breakdown, see Yascha Mounk, *The People vs. Democracy: Why Our Freedom Is in Danger and How to Save It* (Cambridge, MA: Harvard University Press, 2018).

Chapter 3: The birth of authoritarian regimes

For classic case studies of democratic breakdown, see Juan J. Linz and Alfred Stepan, eds., *The Breakdown of Democratic Regimes: Europe* (Baltimore: The Johns Hopkins University Press, 1978); and Juan J. Linz and Alfred Stepan, eds., *The Breakdown of Democratic Regimes: Latin America* (Baltimore: The Johns Hopkins University Press, 1978).

On the politics of hunter-gatherer societies, and the historical rarity of democracy in larger-scale societies, see Francis Fukuyama, *The Origins of Political Order: From Prehuman Times to the French Revolution* (New York: Farrar, Straus and Giroux, 2011).

On polarization, see Thomas Carothers and Andrew O'Donohue, eds., *Democracies Divided: The Global Challenge of Political Polarization* (Washington, D.C.: Brookings Institution Press, 2019); and Milan W. Svolik, "Polarization versus Democracy," *Journal of Democracy*, 30, 3 (2019). On negative partisanship, see Alan I. Abramowitz and Steven W. Webster, "Negative Partisanship: Why Americans Dislike Parties But Behave Like Rabid Partisans," *Political Psychology*, 39, 1 (2018).

Chapter 4: The life of authoritarian regimes

On informal institutions, see Gretchen Helmke and Steven Levitsky, eds., *Informal Institutions and Democracy: Lessons from Latin America* (Baltimore: The Johns Hopkins University Press, 2006). On the "*dedazo*" in Mexico, see chapter by Joy Langston.

On progress in the study of authoritarianism, see David Art, "Review Article: What Do We Know About Authoritarianism After Ten Years?" *Comparative Politics*, 44, 3 (2012). Much of this literature focuses on the role of formal institutions such as political parties and legislatures. See, for example, Jason Brownlee, *Authoritarianism in an Age of Democratization* (New York: Cambridge University Press, 2007); and Jennifer Gandhi, *Political*

Institutions Under Dictatorship (New York: Cambridge University Press, 2008). On the role of coercion, see Sheena Chestnut Greitens, *Dictators and Their Secret Police: Coercive Institutions and State Violence* (New York: Cambridge University Press, 2016).

Chapter 5: The death of authoritarian regimes

For a defense of modernization theory against its critics, see Daniel Treisman, "Economic Development and Democracy: Predispositions and Triggers," *Annual Review of Political Science*, 23 (2020). On how this theory has guided U.S. foreign policy, see Nils Gilman, *Mandarins of the Future: Modernization Theory in Cold War America* (Baltimore: The Johns Hopkins University Press, 2003).

On economic crisis and democratization, see Stephan Haggard and Robert R. Kaufman, *The Political Economy of Democratic Transitions* (Princeton: Princeton University Press, 1995).

On popular struggles for democracy in the Philippines, Poland, and South Africa, see chapters in Adam Roberts and Timothy Garton Ash, eds., *Civil Resistance and Power Politics: The Experience of Non-Violent Action from Gandhi to the Present* (New York: Oxford University Press, 2009).

On U.S. efforts to destabilize democracy in Chile, and later to promote democracy in the country, see Peter Kornbluh, *The Pinochet File: A Declassified Dossier on Atrocity and Accountability* (New York: The New Press, 2003).

On perestroika, glasnost, and the collapse of the Soviet Union, see Michael McFaul, *Russia's Unfinished Revolution: Political Change from Gorbachev to Putin* (Ithaca, NY: Cornell University Press, 2001).

For an overview of Mandela's life, see Elleke Boehmer, *Nelson Mandela: A Very Short Introduction* (Oxford: Oxford University Press, 2008).

On Venezuela's pacted transition to democracy, see Terry Lynn Karl, "Petroleum and Political Pacts: The Transition to Democracy in Venezuela," in Guillermo O'Donnell, Philippe C. Schmitter, and Laurence Whitehead, eds., *Transitions from Authoritarian Rule: Latin America* (Baltimore: The Johns Hopkins University Press, 1986). On South Africa, see chapter 7 of Elisabeth Jean Wood, *Forging Democracy from Below: Insurgent Transitions in South Africa and El Salvador* (New York: Cambridge University Press, 2000).

Chapter 6: The puzzle of authoritarian durability

For a critical overview of theories of culture and democracy, see
chapter 1 of Larry Diamond, *The Spirit of Democracy: The Struggle
to Build Free Societies Throughout the World* (New York: Times
Books/Henry Holt and Company, 2008). On the Arab Spring, see
Jason Brownlee, Tarek Masoud, and Andrew Reynolds, *The Arab
Spring: Pathways of Repression and Reform* (Oxford: Oxford
University Press, 2015).

On the resource curse, see Terry Lynn Karl, *The Paradox of Plenty:
Oil Booms and Petro-States* (Berkeley: University of California
Press, 1997); and Michael L. Ross, *The Oil Curse: How Petroleum
Wealth Shapes the Development of Nations* (Princeton: Princeton
University Press, 2012).

On U.S. democracy promotion, see Thomas Carothers, *Critical Mission:
Essays on Democracy Promotion* (Washington, D.C.: Carnegie
Endowment for International Peace). On authoritarian learning,
see Stephen G. F. Hall, *The Authoritarian International: Tracing
How Authoritarian Regimes Learn in the Post-Soviet Space*
(Cambridge: Cambridge University Press, 2023).

Chapter 7: Legacies of authoritarianism

On human rights violations in Argentina, see Marguerite Feitlowitz,
A Lexicon of Terror: Argentina and the Legacies of Torture
(New York: Oxford University Press, 1998). On Indonesia, see
Geoffrey B. Robinson, *The Killing Season: A History of the
Indonesian Massacres, 1965–66* (Princeton: Princeton University
Press, 2018).

On authoritarian successor parties see chapters in James Loxton and
Scott Mainwaring, eds., *Life After Dictatorship: Authoritarian
Successor Parties Worldwide* (New York: Cambridge University
Press, 2018). On how such parties can help to incorporate potential
democratic "spoilers" into the new regime, see Dan Slater and Joseph
Wong, *From Development to Democracy: The Transformations of
Modern Asia* (Princeton: Princeton University Press, 2022).

On how populists like Hugo Chávez have used constituent assemblies
to entrench themselves in power, see Javier Corrales, *Fixing
Democracy: Why Constitutional Change Often Fails to Enhance
Democracy in Latin America* (New York: Oxford University
Press, 2018).

On the Pinochet saga, see Heraldo Muñoz, *The Dictator's Shadow: Life Under Pinochet* (New York: Basic Books, 2008). On how impunity for human rights abuses was slowly whittled away in Chile, see Cath Collins, *Post-Transitional Justice: Human Rights Trials in Chile and El Salvador* (University Park, PA: Pennsylvania State University Press, 2010).

Index

BEHAVIOURAL ECONOMICS
A Very Short Introduction
Michelle Baddeley

Traditionally economists have based their economic predictions on the assumption that humans are super-rational creatures, using the information we are given efficiently and generally making selfish decisions that work well for us as individuals. Economists also assume that we're doing the very best we can possibly do—not only for today, but over our whole lifetimes too. Increasingly, however, the study of behavioural economics is revealing that our lives are not that simple. Instead, our decisions are complicated by our own psychology. Each of us makes mistakes every day. We don't always know what's best for us and, even if we do, we might not have the self-control to deliver on our best intentions. We struggle to stay on diets, to get enough exercise, and to manage our money.

This *Very Short Introduction* explores the reasons why we make irrational decisions; how we decide quickly; why we make mistakes in risky situations; our tendency to procrastinate; and how we are affected by social influences, personality, mood, and emotions. As Michelle Baddeley explains, the implications of understanding the rationale for our own financial behaviour are huge. She concludes by looking forward, to see what the future of behavioural economics holds for us.

www.oup.com/vsi

BIOGRAPHY
A Very Short Introduction
Hermione Lee

Biography is one of the most popular, best-selling, and widely-read of literary genres. But why do certain people and historical events arouse so much interest? How can biographies be compared with history and works of fiction? Does a biography need to be true? Is it acceptable to omit or conceal things? Does the biographer need to personally know the subject? Must a biographer be subjective? In this *Very Short Introduction* Hermione Lee considers the cultural and historical background of different types of biographies, looking at the factors that affect biographers and whether there are different strategies, ethics, and principles required for writing about one person compared to another. She also considers contemporary biographical publications and considers what kind of 'lives' are the most popular and in demand.

> 'It would be hard to think of anyone better to provide a crisp contribution to OUP's Very Short Introductions.'
>
> **Kathryn Hughes, The Guardian**

CHAOS
A Very Short Introduction
Leonard Smith

Our growing understanding of Chaos Theory is having fascinating applications in the real world - from technology to global warming, politics, human behaviour, and even gambling on the stock market. Leonard Smith shows that we all have an intuitive understanding of chaotic systems. He uses accessible maths and physics (replacing complex equations with simple examples like pendulums, railway lines, and tossing coins) to explain the theory, and points to numerous examples in philosophy and literature (Edgar Allen Poe, Chang-Tzu, Arthur Conan Doyle) that illuminate the problems. The beauty of fractal patterns and their relation to chaos, as well as the history of chaos, and its uses in the real world and implications for the philosophy of science are all discussed in this *Very Short Introduction*.

'... Chaos ... will give you the clearest (but not too painful idea) of the maths involved ... There's a lot packed into this little book, and for such a technical exploration it's surprisingly readable and enjoyable - I really wanted to keep turning the pages. Smith also has some excellent words of wisdom about common misunderstandings of chaos theory ...'

popularscience.co.uk

www.oup.com/vsi

CITIZENSHIP
A Very Short Introduction
Richard Bellamy

Interest in citizenship has never been higher. But what does it mean to be a citizen of a modern, complex community? Why is citizenship important? Can we create citizenship, and can we test for it? In this fascinating Very Short Introduction, Richard Bellamy explores the answers to these questions and more in a clear and accessible way. He approaches the subject from a political perspective, to address the complexities behind the major topical issues. Discussing the main models of citizenship, exploring how ideas of citizenship have changed through time from ancient Greece to the present, and examining notions of rights and democracy, he reveals the irreducibly political nature of citizenship today.

> 'Citizenship is a vast subject for a short introduction, but Richard Bellamy has risen to the challenge with aplomb.'
>
> Mark Garnett, TLS

COMMUNISM
A Very Short Introduction
Leslie Holmes

The collapse of communism was one of the most defining moments of the twentieth century. At its peak, more than a third of the world's population had lived under communist power. What is communism? Where did the idea come from and what attracted people to it? What is the future for communism? This Very Short Introduction considers these questions and more in the search to explore and understand communism. Explaining the theory behind its ideology, and examining the history and mindset behind its political, economic and social structures, Leslie Holmes examines the highs and lows of communist power and its future in today's world.

> Very readable and with its wealth of detail a most valuable reference book.
>
> **Gwyn Griffiths, Morning Star**

www.oup.com/vsi

DEVELOPMENT
A Very Short Introduction
Ian Goldin

What do we mean by development? How can citizens, governments, and the international community foster development?

The process by which nations escape poverty and achieve economic and social progress has been the subject of extensive examination for hundreds of years. The notion of development itself has evolved from an original preoccupation with incomes and economic growth to a much broader understanding of development.

In this *Very Short Introduction* Ian Goldin considers the contributions that education, health, gender, equity, and other dimensions of human well-being make to development, and discusses why it is also necessary to include the role of institutions and the rule of law as well as sustainability and environmental concerns.

DIPLOMACY
A Very Short Introduction
Joseph M. Siracusa

Like making war, diplomacy has been around a very long time, at least since the Bronze Age. It was primitive by today's standards, there were few rules, but it was a recognizable form of diplomacy. Since then, diplomacy has evolved greatly, coming to mean different things, to different persons, at different times, ranging from the elegant to the inelegant. Whatever one's definition, few could doubt that the course and consequences of the major events of modern international diplomacy have shaped and changed the global world in which we live. Joseph M. Siracusa introduces the subject of diplomacy from a historical perspective, providing examples from significant historical phases and episodes to illustrate the art of diplomacy in action.

'Professor Siracusa provides a lively introduction to diplomacy through the perspective of history.'

Gerry Woodard, Senior Fellow in Political Science at the University of Melbourne and former Australasian Ambassador in Asia

www.oup.com/vsi

FREE SPEECH
A Very Short Introduction
Nigel Warburton

'I disapprove of what you say, but I will defend to the death your right to say it' This slogan, attributed to Voltaire, is frequently quoted by defenders of free speech. Yet it is rare to find anyone prepared to defend all expression in every circumstance, especially if the views expressed incite violence. So where do the limits lie? What is the real value of free speech? Here, Nigel Warburton offers a concise guide to important questions facing modern society about the value and limits of free speech: Where should a civilized society draw the line? Should we be free to offend other people's religion? Are there good grounds for censoring pornography? Has the Internet changed everything? This Very Short Introduction is a thought-provoking, accessible, and up-to-date examination of the liberal assumption that free speech is worth preserving at any cost.

'The genius of Nigel Warburton's *Free Speech* lies not only in its extraordinary clarity and incisiveness. Just as important is the way Warburton addresses freedom of speech - and attempts to stifle it - as an issue for the 21st century. More than ever, we need this book.'

Denis Dutton, University of Canterbury, New Zealand

www.oup.com/vsi

GLOBALIZATION
A Very Short Introduction
Manfred Steger

'Globalization' has become one of the defining buzzwords of our time - a term that describes a variety of accelerating economic, political, cultural, ideological, and environmental processes that are rapidly altering our experience of the world. It is by its nature a dynamic topic - and this *Very Short Introduction* has been fully updated for 2009, to include developments in global politics, the impact of terrorism, and environmental issues. Presenting globalization in accessible language as a multifaceted process encompassing global, regional, and local aspects of social life, Manfred B. Steger looks at its causes and effects, examines whether it is a new phenomenon, and explores the question of whether, ultimately, globalization is a good or a bad thing.

LAW
A Very Short Introduction
Raymond Wacks

Law underlies our society - it protects our rights, imposes duties on each of us, and establishes a framework for the conduct of almost every social, political, and economic activity. The punishment of crime, compensation of the injured, and the enforcement of contracts are merely some of the tasks of a modern legal system. It also strives to achieve justice, promote freedom, and protect our security. This *Very Short Introduction* provides a clear, jargon-free account of modern legal systems, explaining how the law works both in the Western tradition and around the world.